M000224269

For Don,
Without whom these pages would be white.

With special gratitude and admiration
for Priya Venkatesh,
Whose brilliance sparks and sustains great things.

The Color Guide to Life: Know and Live Your True Self
Published by Don Lowry and Erica W. Lowry

ISBN: 978-0-9905304-0-4

© 2014, Don Lowry and Erica W. Lowry

Written and developed by Erica W. Lowry, based upon the original work of Don Lowry, creator of "True Colors." The materials herein, trade name and trademarks and all ownership rights thereof are 100% vested and remain vested in Donald and Erica Lowry and the use of these materials, related assessments, training and other corporate modules, and consumer engagement/preferencing and other engagement and entertainment modules, and all content connected therewith is not an assignment, license, or transfer of any rights in and to "True Colors 24" or "True Colors." The "True Colors" brand includes the trade name "True Colors" and all trademarks registered including "True Colors," "True Colors University," "Reading Colors," and the circular logo consisting of orange, gold, green, and blue colors.

All rights reserved. No part of this may be reproduced or transmitted in any form or by any means, electronic or mechanical, including photocopying, recording, scanning or use of any other information storage or retrieval system, without permission of **Don Lowry and Erica W. Lowry.**

Table of Contents

Introduction

In 1979, Don Lowry created True Colors™ to celebrate our individual differences, with an easy language that enables people to share in a positive self- and mutual understanding. While it begins with the understanding of one's self first and foremost, the application of True Colors also enhances one's relationships, and one's success wherever True Colors is applied. Don's intention was to create a model within which everyone could become self-actualized within a system—a community, a school, a family, or an organization—that esteems each participant for who they really are, treats everyone they way they want and need to be treated, and encourages everyone to contribute what they really want to contribute, based on their intrinsic strengths.

Understanding True Colors on one's own, is like receiving a personal gift. You'll begin to notice, as you read through this Guide, that nearly everything that you think and feel, say and do, believe and desire is a part of the answer to the big question, "Who am I?"

You'll start to recognize how all of your own behaviors and choices (past and present) make more sense to you, in terms of who you are—that is, your "True Colors." You'll notice that even past choices, some of which perhaps you may wish you didn't make, were based on a system of values and needs that are intrinsically "you," trying your best to be "you," given the circumstances you were experiencing at the time. . . . As you read, you'll recognize the True Colors of your immediate family, and thereby better understand the family dynamics that you were raised with. As you learn more about each of the Colors, and about your own "True Colors Spectrum," you'll be better able to make choices based on your natural strengths, values, and motivations. They'll become a part of your everyday awareness. What this brings, is greater self-confidence, and a more self-determined life. In a sense, you'll develop your own, inner "Color Guide" that will give you an instinct for what you really need in life, and what's just right for you, and why. . . . This isn't something you have to work at. It just happens naturally, as you use True Colors.

This Guide is also a fun way to learn about other people. Do you ever wonder why your spouse or significant other, your friends and co-workers, and others in your life, are the way they are? Do you want to know what motivates them, what makes them tick? A better understanding of everyone you know is at your fingertips in this Guide. You can easily refer to each Color section, when you want to gain insight into someone you know, or someone you meet.

If you can't guess someone else's Colors, just share the True Colors Cards with them. Ask them to put the Cards in order for themselves, from "Most Like Me" to "Least Like Me." Don't tell them your guess as to their Colors, though—their True Colors are up to them, just as your True Colors are up to you.

The benefit of knowing others' True Colors is not just an increased understanding of others, but a way to actually improve your relationships. When you know someone's True Colors, you know what they want out of life. You know what they value, what they need, how they want to be treated, what causes them stress, and what their strengths are.

The biggest gift of True Colors, happens when you share True Colors with everyone you know. That's when Don Lowry's original purpose for True Colors comes shining through. Those you share True Colors with develop their own inner "Color Guide," that leads them to an understanding about human relationships, that goes well beyond the "Golden Rule" ("Treat others, as you yourself would be treated"), quite surpasses the so-called "Platinum Rule," ("Treat others, they way they want to be treated"), and introduces an even higher truth, shared among those who know and practice True Colors: "Treat others, according to their true selves, because it's best for them, best for me, and best for everyone."

Once you begin to use this Guide, you'll soon find that that's true. When you value others for who they really are, they will contribute their utmost, and they'll also value you, for who you are—and treat you accordingly. You'll realize that you can't possibly do, without our differences. That in fact, none of us can. . . . And those you introduce True Colors to, will start treating others with the same respect and appreciation, for how very different we all are.

But as with all great things in this world, it starts with just one person. In this case, it happens to be you.

Erica W. Lowry

Discover Your True Colors!
The True Colors Card Sort

This book contains four True Colors Cards, which you'll use to begin to determine your True Colors Spectrum.

Take some time to examine the Cards closely, both front and back. You'll notice that the images and the words signify different sets of values, characteristics, and behavioral tendencies. You may find that each Card describes some qualities that you identify with—that's because we each have all four Colors in us.

With that in mind, order the Cards according to "Most Like You" to "Least Like You," placing them from left to right in the order you decide. . . . Consider how you really know yourself to be, how you truly see yourself, rather than how you prefer to present yourself.

Here's an example of how someone might order the cards:

First Card   Second Card   Third Card   Fourth Card

Once you've put your own Cards in order, write down your best estimate as to the order of your Colors, below:

_____ _____ _____ _____

Most like me   A lot like me   Somewhat like me   Least like me

Now, to verify your True Colors, take the Word Cluster Sort Quiz. It will take you about five to seven minutes.

Word Cluster Sort

In the short quiz on the next page, there are clusters of words printed horizontally, within rectangular boxes. Read the four clusters of words shown in each box. Within each box, decide which of the clusters of words best represents you.

Next to the letter at the bottom of each cluster of words, rank the clusters in that box from 4 – 1. Score each cluster of words by giving yourself a "4" for the cluster of words MOST like you, a "3" for the group of words that are next most like you, a "2" for the words that are next most like you, and a "1" for the word cluster that's LEAST like you. Use the same process for the word clusters in each box.

Here is an example:

CONCERNED PROCEDURAL RESPECTFUL	FLEXIBLE DARING IMPULSIVE	OPTIMISTIC HARMONIOUS INSPIRATIONAL	COMPLEX COMPOSED DETERMINED
M _3_	N _1_	O _2_	P _4_

Remember that there are no wrong answers. How you see yourself, is entirely up to you. When you answer, keep in mind how you see yourself overall—not just at work, at home, at school, or with friends—but the whole, "true you," as you know yourself to be.

Take your time. Some of the choices can be difficult, because we each embody a combination of many, many attributes. The key is, do your best to judge each word cluster by the whole cluster of words, not just one word.

Be as honest with yourself as you can, to make sure that your results are accurate.

Word Cluster Sort

Remember: A "**4**" is for "**Most like you,**" while a "**1**" is for "**Least like you**".

SPONTANEOUS HANDS-ON ADVENTURESOME A _____	STABLE RESPONSIBLE TRADITIONAL B _____	AUTHENTIC IMAGINATIVE COMPASSIONATE C _____	INVENTIVE VERSATILE STRATEGIC D _____

CURIOUS CONCEPTUAL KNOWLEDABLE E _____	KIND EMPATHETHIC COMMUNICATIVE F _____	SENSIBLE PRACTICAL DEPENDABLE G _____	IMPACTFUL COMPETITIVE DYNAMIC H _____

LOYAL ORGANIZED DEDICATED I _____	VISIONARY INGENIOUS THEORETICAL J _____	DO-IT-NOW OPEN-MINDED FUNNY K _____	WARM SINCERE THOUGHTFUL L _____

CONCERNED PROCEDURAL RESPECTFUL M _____	FLEXIBLE DARING IMPULSIVE N _____	OPTIMISTIC HARMONIOUS INSPIRATIONAL O _____	COMPLEX COMPOSED DETERMINED P _____

ANALYTICAL PRINCIPLED PHILOSOPHICAL Q _____	CREATIVE SYMPATHETIC AFFECTIONATE R _____	RESOURCEFUL EXCITING COURAGEOUS S _____	PRESERVING ORDERLY HONORABLE T _____

Total the score for these
word clusters: A, H, K, N, S = _____ (Orange)

Total the score for these
word clusters: B, G, I, M, T = _____ (Gold)

Total the score for these
word clusters: C, F, L, O, R = _____ **(Blue)**

Total the score for these
word clusters: D, E, J, P, Q = _____ (Green)

Now, you'll add the results from your True Colors Card Sort, to those of your Word Cluster Sort, to finalize your True Colors Spectrum.

First -- according to your Card Sort, give each Color Card a score, where your 1st Card gets a 4, your 2nd Card gets a 3, your 3rd Card gets a 2, and your 4th Card gets a 1.

Green : .... _____

Orange : .... _____

Gold : .... _____

Blue : .... _____

Add these numbered Card Sort results, to your Word Cluster Sort results, from the previous page:

Green : .... _____

Orange : .... _____

Gold : .... _____

Blue : .... _____

Below, write down your True Colors Spectrum from highest to lowest, according to your combined scores:

_____ ,
_____ ,
_____ ,
_____

Congratulations! You've discovered your True Colors!

The highest possible score for any Color, is 24. The lowest possible score for any Color, is 6. Your scores for each Color give you an idea of how much the values and strengths of each Color influence you, in your character. People who use True Colors often speak of having a "*high* Blue," or a "*low* Gold"—or a "*bright* Orange," or a "*pale* Green." It's a kind of shorthand that everyone who uses True Colors, becomes fluent in fairly quickly.

In the following sections, read about each of the Colors in your Spectrum. Start with your Brightest Color, of course. At the end of your Brightest Color's section, you'll find a personalized report, describing how each Color in your True Colors Spectrum influences you, depending on the order of the four Colors within your Spectrum. Since there are 24 possible variations of True Colors Spectrum, we call these character descriptions "True Colors 24." They show how you're different from others who share your Brightest Color, and what you have in common with those who share your Brightest and Second Color. You'll notice that even though you may share your first two Colors with some, that the transposition of just your last two Colors makes for highly nuanced, very important differences in your personalities.

Reading each of the Color sections, along with True Colors 24, will also help you to recognize everyone who's in your life—your family, friends, co-workers, and others. You'll be able to understand others' values, strengths, needs, and how they want to be treated—what stresses them most, and how you can best communicate with them, to create a more authentic, happier, and more productive relationship.

Green

 ABSTRACT

 PHILOSOPHICAL

 PRIVATE

 SYSTEMIC

How I See Myself

I am multi-faceted. I see us all as complex, changing, unique individuals who can't be "summed up" in any way. But if I were to say that I lead with certain of my traits, I would say that my intellect comes first. My capacities for assessment and analysis allow me to bring some of my greatest strengths to the table—particularly in the areas of innovation, and the invention or improvement of systems.

In order to bring my strengths to bear, I often require time alone to work independently. I enjoy this time to focus my concentration on my chosen task without distraction. Once I've begun a project that holds my interest, I am determined to see it through to completion in a comprehensive manner. It doesn't matter how much time it takes, or who may object to the amount of time I spend. New and constructive concepts and practices are my reward, for my hard work. Because I need this time to think, I do not like to be hurried, or disturbed too frequently. (This is particularly the case, if those disturbances concern the details of matters with which I am not currently concerned.)

Some people may sometimes find me aloof or unemotional, but as they say, "still waters run deep." I am usually busy thinking, while observing the world—and listening. It is helpful to me if people understand this about me. I find that some people, who misunderstand me emotionally, respond as though they themselves are "hurt" by my lack of frequent expression of feelings. It is best for me, if people understand that my lack of outward emotional display is not a reflection of my lack of appreciation of others, because this is simply not the case. I very often consider the positive traits of others, and I appreciate what others contribute to my life. In turn, I do not expect others to constantly provide me with praise. (In fact, I prefer this not to be the case.) I suppose that this is an aspect of my independent nature.

© Erica W. Lowry & Don Lowry, 2014. www.donlowry.com

Because I have always been a person who thinks independently, I am also willing to question authority and existing systems, without any qualms. I have always done so, to some degree, even as a child—not necessarily in order to challenge others, but simply because I may happen to see a better way of thinking about or doing certain things.

In such cases I usually prefer to go my own way, content to invent something new and better, to get things done. I've found this method works well for me.

"I am most excited about learning new things."

"I value individuality, integrity, originality and new ideas."

The Color Guide to Life
© Erica W. Lowry & Don Lowry, 2014. www.donlowry.com

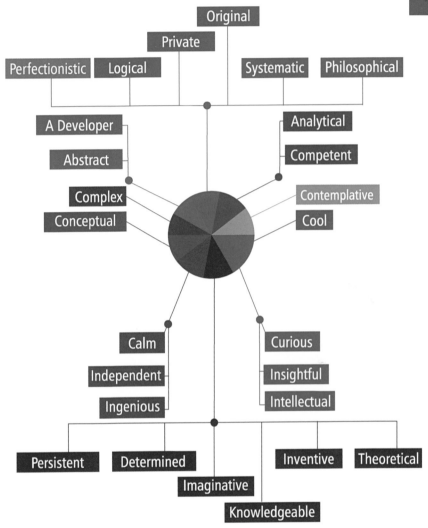

Original
Private
Perfectionistic | Logical | Systematic | Philosophical
A Developer | Analytical
Abstract | Competent
Complex | Contemplative
Conceptual | Cool
Calm | Curious
Independent | Insightful
Ingenious | Intellectual
Persistent | Determined | Inventive | Theoretical
Imaginative
Knowledgeable

Understand that I am

most positive, when you acknowledge and support how I see myself.

The Color Guide to Life
© Erica W. Lowry & Don Lowry, 2014. www.donlowry.com

"My greatest everyday stress occurs when I am prevented from thinking my thoughts through, and implementing my ideas."

What it means to be GREEN

▶ **I like to think about how** I can integrate or implement new concepts, invent new ways of doing things, or improve existing systems.

▶ **My ideal role** is to conceptualize, strategize, problem-solve, innovate, and invent.

▶ **I will continue to be an active participant** if you use my ideas, and give me credit for them.

▶ **I naturally sustain and promote** individuality, integrity, and originality, new ideas and improved systems.

▶ **I am least likely to respond** to pressure to conform, particularly if rules or policies do not make rational sense to me.

▶ **I want relationships that** are interesting, where I can brainstorm with others and expand ideas, to move matters forward.

▶ **You will lose my attention if you** don't challenge my intellect, respect my ideas, or if you offer too much small talk.

▶ **Things I don't enjoy are** having to repeat myself, or repeat tasks; I don't enjoy having to show emotion publicly; I don't enjoy handling the routine details of daily life, because I prefer to focus on the big picture.

▶ **I feel strongest about myself when** I am designing new and better systems, from a global perspective.

▶ **My greatest everyday stress** occurs when I am prevented from thinking my thoughts through, and from moving forward in implementing my ideas. This occurs when I am overloaded with things to do that are mundane. These mundane tasks include having to handle record-keeping; particularly stressful is having to prove that I am doing what I say I am doing.

▶ **If I am stressed, or in a bad mood, you need to:** Give me space and time alone to think things through, and in conversation, speak calmly and rationally with me, without displays of emotion.

▶ **My greatest fear** is incompetence. I always need to be in a position where I know what I am doing, and why. This is one of the reasons why I like to gather so much knowledge—other than the fact that knowledge is interesting.

▶ **I like my spiritual life to be** private and individualistic.

▶ **In a love relationship, I tend** to enjoy a partner who understands and appreciates my ideas, with whom I can have interesting conversations. I don't much enjoy public displays of affection, because I like to keep those things private.

The best way to engage me is by:

▶ Not expecting too much small talk

▶ Seeking out my logic and my ideas

▶ Respecting my intellect and my analytical abilities

▶ Giving me information I need, and giving me the time alone to analyze it, and conduct further research; I need time to think things through, thoroughly

▶ Offering to handle details, which is hugely appreciated

"I am most content when my intellect is engaged in the beauty of a welcome challenge."

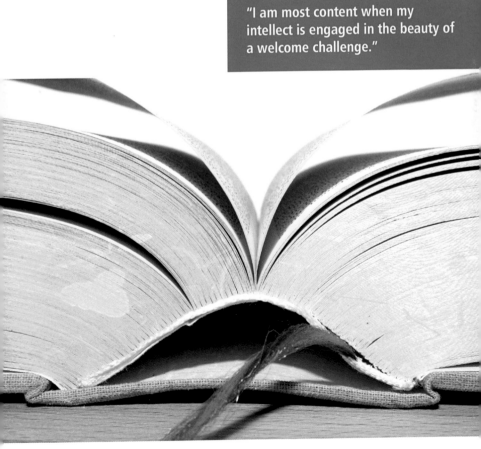

My Success at Work

I function best in an environment where:

▶ I can adapt tasks to my way of accomplishing things

▶ I can choose my own tasks

▶ I can analyze and innovate

▶ I can improve upon existing material or existing systems

▶ I have private space to work

▶ It is quiet, with few interruptions

▶ There is an interesting variety of things to work on

▶ I feel valued for my intellect and ideas

▶ There are no emotional outbursts

"Please understand that I often see things from a different perspective."

What's my Change Style?

The pace of change has accelerated, and shows no sign of slowing down. "Disruption" of existing industries, and higher expectations to continually innovate and adapt, have become the norm. Whether or not you take an active role in creating change yourself, we all participate in the new normal. So it's key to have an understanding of change. It happens in stages, and different kinds of people with very different strengths are needed at every stage, in order for change to succeed and be sustained.

You have an optimal, essential role. What are Greens' natural strengths, in each stage of enacting change?

In conceiving of the need for change . . .

▶ Greens begin with their intrinsic passion for *innovating, brainstorming,* and *expanding on ideas*.

In developing change concepts . . .

▶ Greens dig into the processes of *envisioning, theorizing, and researching possibilities*.

In finalizing change concepts . . .

▶ Greens will continue to *experiment, integrate various ideas and practices, and analyze different outcomes*.

In enacting change . . .

▶ Greens will *consult and deliberate* with others, and will continue to be *perfecting, perfecting, and perfecting* any change that they've been part of. But they prefer to let others sustain the routine operations, of any new system.

The Color Guide to Life
© Erica W. Lowry & Don Lowry, 2014. www.donlowry.com

Communicating with Me

Remember: Do not repeat anything with me, I heard you the first time. . . . I repeat; do not repeat anything with me.

Your Ideal Approach: Respect my mind and my ideas, and my privacy.

Your Ideal Tone: Calm, thoughtful, objective, reasonable.

Your Ideal Topics: Ideas - especially new, interesting ideas.

Your Ideal Openers - Asking for Thoughts and Ideas:

▶ "I'd like to know if you can you help me figure out . . ."

▶ "I've got some research that I'd like to get your opinion on."

▶ "I want to pick your brain. Can you help me with your ideas about . . ."

▶ "I've been thinking about _____, and I wonder if you could offer your thoughts."

Your Ideal Rebuttals - Respecting Ideas, and The Debate Process:

▶ "Now that's really interesting. I didn't see it from that perspective. _____ has a different idea, which is _____. I wonder what your thoughts are."

▶ "I came at this from a different angle, which took into consideration . . ."

▶ "I really appreciate your thoughts about that. So what do you think of my idea that . . ."

▶ "It's interesting that you see it that way. What would you think, about a next step that incorporates my ideas about . . ."

The Color Guide to Life
© Erica W. Lowry & Don Lowry, 2014. www.donlowry.com

▶ "I understand that this is contrary to the way you normally think. But it would be great if you could spend some time thinking about . . ."

▶ **Your Ideal Praise** - About My Intellect - Keep it Short and Sweet

▶ "Sometimes, talking to you is like taking the blinders off."

▶ "I always feel a little smarter after talking to you."

▶ "Fascinating! Where did you learn about that?"

▶ "That was just brilliant. . . . How did you figure that out?"

Your Ideal Humor: Irony, puns, intellectual humor, wry or dry humor. Preferably, combined.

Never, Ever: Ask personal questions without sufficient warning, and be sure never to mistakenly malign a Green person's intelligence or competence.

"Sometimes talking to you is like taking the blinders off."

What I have in Common WITH OTHER COLORS

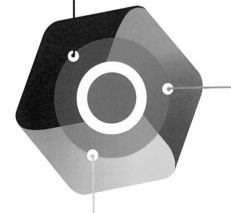

Like Blues,

I tend to think abstractly, and I have a streak of idealism. We share a need to improve the world and the lives of others in a way that incorporates an all-inclusive, intuitive approach.

Like Oranges,

I love variety and flexibility, and I'm easily bored. We share the strength of inventiveness, and a love of change.

Like Golds,

I can be very detail-oriented, and I'm determined to work toward perfect completion. I enjoy doing research like those who are Gold, and we share a love of privacy.

The Color Guide to Life
© Erica W. Lowry & Don Lowry, 2014. www.donlowry.com

My Health and Wellness

In order to be healthy, my own needs and values must be incorporated into any health and wellness process. I also need to be able to use my personal strengths, in becoming and staying healthy. As a GREEN, any health and wellness program I participate in has to ENGAGE MY INTELLECT in A VARIETY OF WAYS, or I'll tend not to stay with it. Concerning my own health and wellness, I need to be able to make decisions based upon:

▶ First analyzing information, such as scientific research

▶ Having the freedom to make my own choices, and go my own direction

▶ Getting time alone, which I know improves my well-being

▶ Having an interesting variety of options, in terms of diet and/or exercise

▶ Whether or not I will get bored (by exercise, by other people, by time spent waiting)

▶ My need for open space and light, wherever I get exercise

As a Green, I need to be aware of:

▶ Being unconscious of my physical health, due to work needs

▶ The time I spend sitting at a desk; I need to schedule regular walking/movement breaks

▶ Finding ways to make exercise *interesting*, every time

▶ The fact that *boredom* is what may cause me to overeat

I like to learn about health information by:

▶ Reading about it in books and periodicals I trust

▶ Reading about interesting new advances, on the Internet

▶ Viewing scholarly lectures online

What will motivate me to improve my health and wellness:

▶ An innovative, effective, interesting, research-based approach

▶ No waste of time (such as time spent driving, or waiting, or talking)

▶ Plenty of personal space and light

▶ Change and variety in a program

▶ Explanation from an expert

"I need open space, light, and time alone to think."

© Erica W. Lowry & Don Lowry, 2014. www.donlowry.com

My Primary Causes of Stress

▶ Not being able to set my own standards in life

▶ No time or space alone

▶ Boredom at work and in life

▶ Injustice

▶ Lack of control

▶ Nonsensical rules

▶ Being forced to follow others' set routines

▶ Having to deal with others' emotional trauma, too often

▶ Putting too much work on my plate

When I am very stressed I tend to:

▶ Become cynical or sarcastic

▶ Need to escape or withdraw emotionally

▶ Become perfectionistic, a "workaholic"

▶ Become indecisive

▶ Tend to micromanage others

Please Don't:

- ▶ Rush me
- ▶ Insult my intelligence
- ▶ Interrupt me in my work, too often
- ▶ Withhold information I may need
- ▶ Expect me to follow rules that don't make sense
- ▶ Ask me to do the same task repeatedly
- ▶ Invade my privacy
- ▶ Overload me with emotional input

"Please don't ask me to do the same task repeatedly."

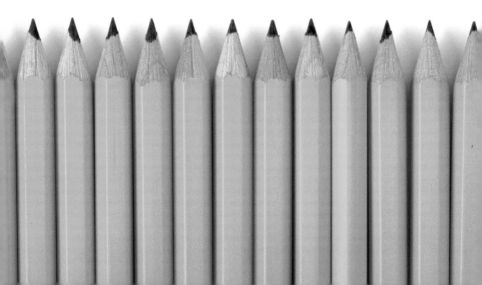

Tips: Daily Happiness for Greens

▶ The key to my happiness, is being able to envisage and invent things that make a difference. If I find that my life is "missing something," it's usually that. I need to be inventing, every day.

▶ I need to make sure that I have some purely autonomous time and space every day—even if it's just 20 minutes of aloneness.

▶ Even though I'm a perfectionist, and I see nothing wrong with perfectionism, sometimes it's best to recall that letting perfection get in the way of the good . . . is bad.

▶ Even though I'm highly independent, asking for help and input from others does not in any way signal any level of incompetence in me. Quite the opposite, it means that I'm confident in my own abilities and know that asking others for input, increases buy-in overall.

▶ It's best for me in the long run, if I can let others know that my lack of outward emotional display is not a reflection of my lack of emotion.

▶ In my relationships with friends, family, co-workers, and any significant other, saying "please" and "thank you" whenever they're called for is the simplest way to lower stress in my relationships, increase everyone's effectiveness . . . and increase others' willingness to give me the autonomy I seek!

"My lack of outward emotional display does not reflect a lack of emotion.

"...Still waters run deep."

There are 24 possible variations of True Colors Spectrum. Which one are you?

You are Green/Orange/Blue/Gold . . .

The world needs change-agents like you.

At your best, you improve things that impact a lot of people, and you create entirely new systems. Your determination to make a better world knows no bounds. While you enjoy brainstorming with those you respect, you love solitary time in order to develop your ideas. Your inventions may involve something abstract, appealing to your Green side, or something concrete, appealing to your Orange side. Whatever it is you invent, you intend to impact a multitude of people.

© Erica W. Lowry & Don Lowry, 2014. www.donlowry.com

Being Green, you like to think things through before you act. You seek perfection, and hate to make mistakes. But your Orange side is willing to take big risks, and thrives on taking immediate action. This combustive combination drives the engine that moves you toward achieving great things. But it can also be a source of inner-conflict, and a source of stress for yourself and others. You can learn to balance your need for perfection, and your need for taking immediate action, by keeping your sense of humor.

As a Green/Orange/Blue/Gold, you tend to be a visionary, with a passion to make an impact on society. But you can also have a tendency to be generous to a fault, and you have some difficulty staying organized. Being Green/Orange, you're likely to tackle a lot of challenging, exciting goals; you may underestimate all of the details that may need to be taken care of. You can either improve your organizational skills - that is, "brighten your Gold," or get help from others who are higher Gold than you are.

Your incisive management skills are
softened by a warm, steady nature.

Your Green talents for innovation and global thinking are motivated by your Gold gifts for creating organization and stability. And so you're likely to be drawn to opportunities that will allow you to have the authority to run systems. This may involve managing money, people, information, product or machinery, or all of the above. You excel at understanding and managing the intricacies of large systems. Your keen eye for what's practical steers you away from doing anything unwise.

Being Green first, you also like to invent new systems. With Gold second, you're likely to plan well in advance, which usually spells success. As a Green/Gold, you're likely to take a scientific approach to everything you do: you research to find the facts, hypothesize using your research, and only experiment (or invent) based upon known criteria. If there may be loss, you plan for it. You are methodical in reaching time-sensitive goals, with anticipated results. For you, inner conflict only arises when your desire to invent clashes with your desire to follow the rules.

As a Green/Gold/Blue/Orange, you will want to be part of running an organization that helps people - or you'll want to create that organization, even as a company of one. You work extremely well on your own. You're an unusually calm, stable, pensive, and practical person - you're not one to ruffle other's feathers, in reaching your goals. Nor do you put yourself in situations where you risk doing so. Rather, you proceed like a careful, knowledgeable surgeon with an impeccable bedside manner. With Orange last, you may not always stand up for your ideas when you should; your original ideas certainly warrant standing up for.

You're a steady, calm, creative and thorough innovator.

Your Green drive to learn, invent and improve upon things is motivated by your strong Blue need to help others. Both Green and Blue signal extreme sensitivity to the abstract nuances of the world, and the inner-workings of things and people, and so you're likely to be attracted to systems of thought and activities that serve the world, in very a specific, sophisticated fashion. And so you're likely to want to fine-tune, enhance, and perfect systems or activities through your Green gift of innovation. At your best, you can invent entirely new systems or activities or methods that will help quite a lot of people.

Being Green/Blue means that you're likely to engage in highly abstract thought. You love to talk about ideas, and to philosophize. Others may even find that sometimes, you're a little too abstract—you'll need to be a bit more concrete, for some. You'll also find that your Green need to be the sole and original author of your ideas sometimes conflicts with your Blue need to be emotionally supportive and nurturing of others.

As a Green/Blue/Gold/Orange, your sensitive, patient nature allows you to innovate and be of service calmly and steadily, always seeing things through to completion. You're not a boisterous person, but you're an excellent and interested listener, so people find you very easy to get along with. With Orange as your last Color, you're not likely to want to compete, or leap into center stage, which you could sometimes benefit from. And although you are a highly gifted innovator, you may not seize on opportunities that you deserve. It may serve you to remember to brighten your Orange, when unusual opportunities come your way. Opportunities that may seem daunting, at first, may be just the right path for your steady creative energies.

You can systematize and oversee the change that the world needs.

At your best, you improve things that impact a lot of people, and you create entirely new systems. Your determination to make a better world knows no bounds. While you enjoy brainstorming with those you respect, you love solitary time in order to develop your ideas. Your inventions may involve something abstract, appealing to your Green side, or something concrete, appealing to your Orange side. Whatever it is you invent, you intend to impact a multitude of people.

© Erica W. Lowry & Don Lowry, 2014. www.donlowry.com

Being Green, you like to think things through before you act. You seek perfection, and hate to make mistakes. But your Orange side is willing to take big risks, and thrives on taking immediate action. This combustive combination drives the engine that moves you toward achieving great things. But it can also be a source of inner-conflict, and a source of stress for yourself and others. You can learn to balance your need for perfection, and your need for taking immediate action, by keeping your sense of humor.

As a Green/Orange/Gold/Blue, you're well-organized in life, but your zeal for order coupled with very high ambition might alienate the very people who are trying to help you— without your even knowing it. Of course, that is not your intent, but you are focused on getting important things done, and you may not be aware of the feelings of those around you. Your third color, Gold, will place higher importance on organization, completion, and procedures, and less on the things that motivate people. In this case, be sure not to overlook one of your greatest assets – the people who can help you achieve your goals.

You can organize and maintain complex, multi-level systems.

Your Green talents for innovation and global thinking are motivated by your Gold gifts for creating organization and stability. And so you're likely to be drawn to opportunities that will allow you to have the authority to run systems. This may involve managing money, people, information, product or machinery, or all of the above. You excel at understanding and managing the intricacies of large systems. Your keen eye for what's practical steers you away from doing anything unwise.

The Color Guide to Life
© Erica W. Lowry & Don Lowry, 2014. www.donlowry.com

Being Green first, you also like to invent new systems. With Gold second, you're likely to plan well in advance, which usually spells success. As a Green/Gold, you're likely to take a scientific approach to everything you do: you research to find the facts, hypothesize using your research, and only experiment (or invent) based upon known criteria. If there may be loss, you plan for it. You are methodical in reaching time-sensitive goals, with anticipated results. For you, inner conflict only arises when your desire to invent clashes with your desire to follow the rules.

As a Green/Gold/Orange/Blue, you are driven to the top tier of your profession. You're not only a global thinker with superlative organizational skills, you have the Orange ability to troubleshoot any problem, and an Orange talent for communicating your ideas with flair. On your way to the top, make sure that you don't neglect the feelings of others, which you may tend to do, with a pale Blue. While you're definitely not a "touchy-feely" type, you can improve relations with others by showing your Orange, humorous side. As a Green/Gold, you have a clever, wry sense of humor.

At your best, your innovations and ideas
serve humanity.

Your Green drive to learn, invent and improve upon things
is motivated by your strong Blue need to help others. Both
Green and Blue signal extreme sensitivity to the abstract
nuances of the world, and the inner-workings of things and
people, and so you're likely to be attracted to systems of
thought and activities that serve the world, in very a specific,

sophisticated fashion. And so you're likely to want to fine-tune, enhance, and perfect systems or activities through your Green gift of innovation. At your best, you can invent entirely new systems or activities or methods that will help quite a lot of people.

Being Green/Blue means that you're likely to engage in highly abstract thought. You love to talk about ideas, and philosophize. Others may even find that sometimes, you're a little too abstract—you'll need to be a bit more concrete, for some. You'll also find that your Green need to be the sole and original author of your ideas sometimes conflicts with your Blue need to be emotionally supportive and nurturing of others.

As a Green/Blue/Orange/Gold, you are the most abstract type of thinker, and with Orange as your third Color, you're highly communicative, innovative, and energetic. You're willing to take risks, in what you decide to invent or improve upon, in your quest to be of service to humanity. You're willing to stand up against opposition, if you think that what you're doing will ultimately be of great assistance. But with a third Orange, you're also likely to become impatient with yourself or others, if you don't get quick results. And being Gold last, impediments will eventually manifest if you don't keep in mind that you must manage the details well, in any endeavor.

© Erica W. Lowry & Don Lowry, 2014. www.donlowry.com

Blue

 PERCEPTIVE

 HARMONIOUS

 NURTURING

 OPTIMISTIC

How I See Myself

If there were a phrase that best describes the way I try to live my life, it would be "To thine own self be true." Since feelings are important to me, I pay attention to them. This means that I also pay close attention to others' feelings, with genuine empathy and compassion. I feel good about helping people (I think we should all help each other)—however sometimes, due to my enthusiasm, I inadvertently help others instead of helping myself. I certainly don't mind this, unless I find myself in a position where I'm ignoring my own needs. If I run into trouble in life—that's usually where the trouble is.

On the positive side, I do very much enjoy seeing people happy and in harmony. As simple as it may sound, it gives me personal joy, to see someone I care for wearing a great big smile. That's why I spend time doing thoughtful things for others—I know how much it can mean. Even if a total stranger shows me the genuine, kind side of his or her nature, and I can share that side of myself too, it's fulfilling, because it reminds me that we're all connected. And so when people I care for have put their time, thought and energy into doing something nice (and thoughtful) for me, well, it sends me over the top. Nothing means more, than to give and receive love.

The essence of my need to help and inspire others, and be inspired, is my need to be connected. I feel that we are all connected spiritually, and that reaching out to others is an extension and an expression of this truth about all of us. I am a spiritual person, and reaching out to others is my way of showing what I believe is our purpose here on earth. I don't think that we can love too much.

And so I am a natural romantic. I believe in love at first sight. I think that it's possible for two people to be soul-mates. Since love is so important to me (as is being true to myself) a

© Erica W. Lowry & Don Lowry, 2014. www.donlowry.com

harmonious, honest, intimate, growing love relationship is a very big priority in my life. I put a lot of energy into making a love relationship work, and I use my strengths of empathy and compassion to help me deeply understand (and even anticipate) another person's needs. Sometimes I put so much energy into a love relationship, that I forget my own needs. I need to remind myself now and then, not to wait too long to ask for what I really want—and to spend some of my creative energy doing things just for myself. I need to make sure I pay attention to my own feelings. Keeping a journal, writing poetry, playing an instrument, or making any form of artwork is a great source of self-expression and growth, for me.

Of all people, I'm the one you can walk up to and get a hug from, pretty much any time. Don't forget, though—I'm also one who loves to get that hug, too.

"It gives me personal joy, to see someone I care for wearing a great big smile."

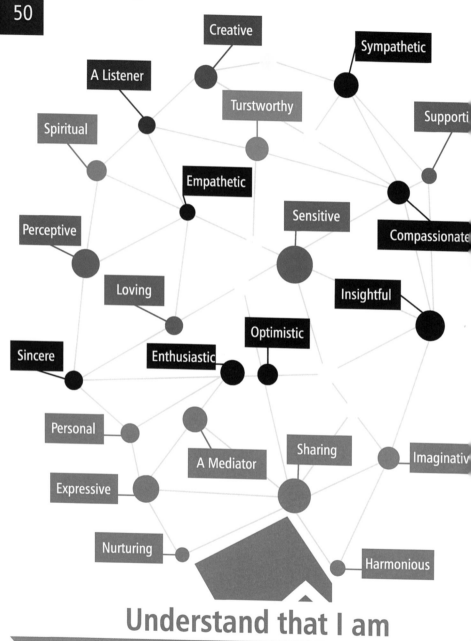

Creative

Sympathetic

A Listener

Turstworthy

Supporti

Spiritual

Empathetic

Sensitive

Supporti

Perceptive

Compassionate

Loving

Insightful

Optimistic

Sincere

Enthusiastic

Personal

A Mediator

Sharing

Imaginativ

Expressive

Nurturing

Harmonious

Understand that I am

most positive, when you acknowledge and support how I see myself.

The Color Guide to Life
© Erica W. Lowry & Don Lowry, 2014. www.donlowry.com

What it means to be BLUE

▶ **I like to think about** how I can help people, and improve my own relationships - and the relationships of others. This goes for all relationships, those at work and outside of work. I also like to think about the creative things that I enjoy doing, both work-related and personal.

▶ **The best way to engage me** is to be open and friendly. Approach me with an expression of your own feelings - and ask me about my own feelings, too.

▶ **I will continue to be an active participant** if I sense that you appreciate my unique contribution, and if you continue to communicate with me in an open manner.

▶ **I naturally sustain and promote** communicative, harmonious relationships.

▶ **I am least likely to respond** to teasing, emotional coldness, or conflict of any kind. Please think through your criticism to ensure that it encompasses empathetic understanding of factors involved - which is what I naturally do for everyone.

▶ **You will lose my attention if you** never discuss or include the human element.

▶ **Things I don't enjoy are** seeing others in emotional pain, or being in emotional pain myself, through feeling rejected, mocked, or unappreciated.

I like my spiritual life to be highly connected, joyous, and gratitude-filled.

The Color Guide to Life
© Erica W. Lowry & Don Lowry, 2014. www.donlowry.com

▶ **I feel strongest about myself when** I can be true to myself—while helping others, and feeling appreciated.

▶ **My greatest everyday stress** occurs when I repeatedly feel helpless in my mission to help others, or when I feel unappreciated.

▶ **If I am stressed, or in a bad mood, you need to**: Ask me about my feelings, welcome my showing you my emotions, and comfort me. It also cheers me up if you do something thoughtful for me, or give me a sincere hug. I want to know that you care about me.

▶ **My greatest fear is** loneliness, or getting my heart broken—or deeply hurting someone else.

▶ **I like my spiritual life to be** highly connective, joyous, and gratitude-filled.

▶ **In a love relationship, I tend to** share my whole self with my partner—my mind, heart, body, and soul. I am a natural romantic. I enjoy expressing love through thoughtful communication in all its forms. Being close and doing things with a partner that show how we truly feel about each other, is like heaven on earth.

The best way to engage me is by:

▶ Being open and friendly

▶ Seek out my feelings on any issue

▶ Offering opportunities for me to be imaginative and creative

▶ Appreciating my contribution—and showing me your appreciation

▶ Helping me to understand a project more fully (not just parts of a project), so that I can help beyond expectations

My Success at Work

I function best in an environment where:

▶ There is little or no conflict - lots of rapport and cooperation

▶ I am free to help, and my contribution makes a difference

▶ I feel like I make a unique contribution, based on who I am

▶ I feel genuinely appreciated by those I work with

▶ I have the ability to be imaginative and creative, to grow personally and professionally

▶ My contribution helps even beyond the workplace

▶ There is a warm, welcoming environment

▶ There is some support for my whole self, not just myself in my role at work

▶ I am able to successfully mediate differences of opinion, to create harmony

What's My Change Style?

The pace of change has accelerated, and shows no sign of slowing down. "Disruption" of existing industries, and higher expectations to continually innovate and adapt, have become the norm. Whether or not you take an active role in creating change yourself, we all participate in the new normal. So it's key to have an understanding of change. It happens in stages, and different kinds of people with very different strengths are needed at every stage, in order for change to succeed and be sustained.

You have an optimal, essential role. What are Blues' natural strengths, in each stage of enacting change?

In conceiving of the need for change . . .

Blues begin with their passion for *inspiring* others, *imagining* new possibilities, and *illuminating* others' ideas and feelings.

In developing change concepts . . .

Blues have a critical role in *intuiting* new ways to think and feel about circumstances, *encouraging* others, and *counseling* others through all difficulties, big and small.

In finalizing change concepts . . .

Blues will continue to *support* everyone involved, *create consensus*, and *empower* everyone to play his or her optimal role.

In enacting change . . .

Blues are there to *facilitate* any and all changes enacted, *nurture* everyone through any changes, and *promote* respectful and friendly relationships at all times—especially when the going gets tough.

Communicating with Me

Remember: As a Blue, I like acknowledgement of my humanity, and yours. I appreciate at least one thoughtful statement in our conversation.

Your Ideal Approach: Seeking the best for all.

Your Ideal Tone: Friendly, warm, open, kind, inspirational, encouraging.

Your Ideal Topics: Your feelings about something, or asking about my feelings about something. . . . For us Blues, the word "feel" means "think" and encompasses both.

Your Ideal Openers: Sincere and Thoughtful

▶ "It is so good to talk to you. I'm wondering what your feelings are, about . . ."

▶ "I'm hoping to send a little inspiration your way, today . . ."

▶ "I'm so glad to get you on the phone. It's good to hear your voice. How did your kid's exam go?" (i.e., a relevant question about some personal event—try to remember family names.)

▶ "Hey, so how are you doing? I've been thinking of you!"

Your Ideal Rebuttals: Honest, about Feelings

▶ "Since I feel differently about that, it would help me to know that you'll listen to what I have to say . . ."

▶ "I'm sad that we disagree. I'd feel a lot better if we could find a way to see eye-to-eye on this. What about . . ."

▶ "I really appreciate your sharing that with me, but I need your understanding, that I feel somewhat differently."

© Erica W. Lowry & Don Lowry, 2014. www.donlowry.com

▶ "I need to be honest with you about my feelings about this …"

Your Ideal Praise: Pointing out His or Her Inner Beauty, Goodness, and Inspirational Abilities

▶ "You're the greatest listener. It makes me feel important."

▶ "Talking to you just lights up my day."

▶ "You know, you really make a difference in my life. You help me in so many thoughtful ways."

▶ "You inspired me to (do a positive thing). Thank you so much, I really appreciated your inspiration."

▶ "Talking to you really cheers me up."

Your Ideal Humor: Goofy jokes about people, so long as they're not harshly denigrating.

Never, Ever: Tease a Blue, as this will not be taken as the least bit funny. It will be more hurtful than you might expect. To a Blue, there is no such thing as "affectionate teasing." There is a whole universe of better ways to demonstrate affection, to a Blue. Never accuse a Blue of being unfeeling, selfish, or "mean." Those are the very last things they'll ever want to be, or be perceived as.

What I have in Common WITH OTHER COLORS

• Like Greens,

I tend to be an intuitive thinker, and I see the value of idealism in helping to change the world for the better.

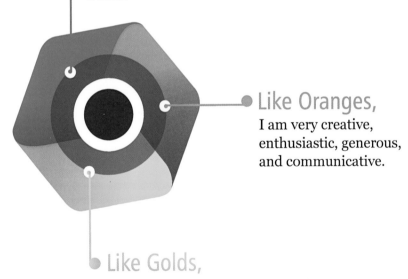

• Like Oranges,

I am very creative, enthusiastic, generous, and communicative.

• Like Golds,

I care very much about the people in my community (both where I live and work) and our helpful service to each other.

© Erica W. Lowry & Don Lowry, 2014. www.donlowry.com

My Health and Wellness

In order to be Healthy, my own needs and values must be incorporated into any health and wellness program. I also need to be able to use my personal strengths, in becoming and staying healthy. As a BLUE, any health and wellness program I engage in has to be INSPIRING, UPLIFTING, and MUTUALLY SUPPORTIVE, or I won't stay with it. I'll be successful in a health and wellness process if I know I can count on:

▶   Feeling emotionally fulfilled and nurtured

▶   Being with friends and family

▶   Supporting others emotionally, and feeling supported

▶   Feeling accepted just as I am

▶   Feeling genuinely encouraged by others

▶   Feeling "centered" and connected spiritually

I need to be aware of:

▶   Allowing my personal relationships and my need to help others distract me from making time for myself, and the things I need to do for my health

"I'm tempted by sweets and comfort food, when I feel that life isn't sweet or comfortable."

- ▶ The fact that I may overeat when I feel lonely, unappreciated, or disconnected from my true self

- ▶ My need to stay spiritually connected, which helps keep me well

- ▶ My social options for physical activity, such as dance, sports, community gardening, or walking or hiking with friends

I consider my health and wellness to be:

- ▶ Important, so that I can help take care of others

- ▶ Something I don't want to tackle all by myself

I like to learn about health information by:

- ▶ Talking with friends and family

- ▶ Watching talk shows that incorporate health and wellness

What will motivate me to improve my health and wellness is:

- ▶ A highly supportive network, where I can help others and they genuinely enjoy helping me

- ▶ A shared attitude of "getting better every day"

- ▶ Gaining a clear vision of my best potential self, in all respects - not just my physical health or appearance

- ▶ Feeling that my improved health and wellness overall, in my body, mind, and spirit, will give me a more emotionally fulfilling life

- ▶ Feeling that my improved health and wellness will help me become stronger, emotionally

My Primary Causes of Stress

▶ Conflict with others

▶ Being out of touch with myself

▶ Others' criticism of me

▶ A feeling of helplessness when others are in pain

▶ Being surrounded by others' conflict

▶ Lack of inspiration in life

▶ Lack of romance and affection

▶ Helping others too much, not getting my own needs met

▶ Not feeling appreciated

When I am very stressed, I tend to:

▶ Have emotional, verbal outbursts, to express my needs

▶ Play the martyr, to make others see the wrong in their ways

▶ Overeat, because food provides the emotional nourishment I seek

▶ Become depressed, and want to hide

▶ Want to cry, to release the emotion

Please Don't:

▶ Alienate me/Ignore me

▶ Tease me

▶ Suppress my creativity

▶ Forget to say "Thank you", once in a while

▶ Raise your voice at me in anger

Tips: Daily Happiness for Blues

▶ Every day, I need to find some time to connect with my feelings—through some form of self-expression or self-exploration . . .. Even if it's only for 20 minutes.

▶ If I'm not getting what I need in my everyday life with others, I need to simply ask what for I need. (My talent for reading others' needs is not shared by everyone.)

▶ If it seems that someone isn't enthusiastic about my contribution, I need to remember that others often express themselves very differently. (Others' lack of expression, or very different way of expressing themselves, is NOT necessarily a reflection of their feelings about me.)

▶ I try to remember that my true self, and what I consider to be the source of all life—as well as every living being-is all *interconnected*. When I remember this, I realize that no matter what conflict or misunderstanding may be occurring - that we're all deeply connected. . . . With this, I can recall that my real purpose and my true self are never lost, due to any pain or conflict.

There are 24 possible variations of True Colors Spectrum. Which one are you?

You are Blue/Gold/Green/Orange . . .

Admit it - you are the support beam that keeps the house standing

Whether others know it or not, you are the one who is making sure that people are getting done what needs to get done, while getting cared for in the ways they need to be cared for. The reason that others may not know this is that you're not likely to blow your own horn. It's only when people take the time to consider who or what is really maintaining so much detailed order and solid effectiveness in the everyday running of things, that they realize that it's you, holding things and people together. You do this because you have the caring, "Blue glue" to accomplish that, while your work ethic is solid Gold. Once people recognize this truth about you, they find you invaluable.

With Blue as your first Color, you do like to socialize, but with Gold as your second Color, you do so only after all the work is done. (It's best if your work includes talking to others!) So when it's time to socialize, you do that with both orderliness, and a warm human touch. This makes you a wonderful host or hostess for traditional celebrations. In fact, in doing anything that involves planning, where people are concerned—you shine. You tend to help keep everyone around you better-organized, through daily acts of thoughtfulness and concern. When others show their appreciation, you rightly enjoy it, although you rarely, if ever, ask for it.

As a Blue/Gold/Green/Orange, you use your inventiveness and insight to come up with creative ways to improve others' lives. You're especially considerate of others' needs, and you're very careful not to hurt others' feelings. You are a spiritual person, who deeply feels the importance of your faith. Family is also at the top of your list, so sharing spiritual traditions with family and friends brings you great joy. You memorialize these important events, to cherish these memories in future. As you make your detailed plans in life, don't forget the rewards of occasional "Orange" spontaneity—sometimes, let yourself be pleased by unexpected events. As a highly spiritual person, you can see how everything ultimately will work for the good —you know that even misadventures in life can provide a long-term benefit for all.

You're a gifted people-person who wants to help others, in ways that you and others can both enjoy and grow from.

With Blue as your Primary Color, you need to create harmony and help others. This is motivated by your Orange desire to help people have fun—and also to have fun, yourself. You have the unusual ability to bring out people's child-like side, which is innocent, vulnerable, and open to anything. In your relationships with others, you're like the icing on the cake—your specialty is to help people be happier and enjoy themselves, through the many thoughtful, fun and creative

© Erica W. Lowry & Don Lowry, 2014. www.donlowry.com

things you love to do. You spend considerable effort coming up with things for people to look forward to, enjoy, and benefit from. For most, this would be a titanic effort—but not for you. It's something you do naturally.

Being Blue first, you're likely to be drawn to a helping profession, but with a second Orange you also need to be in a high energy situation where troubleshooting, creative self-expression, and a good sense of humor come into play. In anything you do, you bring a caring, human touch - and you'll also contribute the playful, creative energy of a child. Trouble enters when people think that because you're such a people-person, that you can't be hurt, which you can be, deeply—due to your very sensitive Blue side. And sometimes, you are caught between your Blue desire to be nurturing to others, and your Orange desire to be center-stage.

As a Blue/Orange/Green/Gold, you're apt to be an idea-factory for brand new ways to help people - or you'll improve upon ways that have worked before, by making them more fun and more personal. This brainstorming just adds to your sense of meaning, in life. While you're inventing new ways for adding more life to people's lives, be sure to pay attention to the details in how to complete your plans. Your pale Gold signifies that you could get tripped up by details that you didn't foresee—so try to plan ahead a little more carefully.

You are Blue/Green/Gold/Orange . . .

You're a serene healer, with the ability to touch the hearts of many.

Your strong desire to help others is achieved through your sensitive, original approach. You are deeply imaginative, and you enjoy creating new ways to be of service to others, in whatever position you find yourself. You enjoy sharing your helpful, unique contributions. In fact, you most enjoy helping others through communication: writing, talking, or artistic expression.

And you probably enjoy reading or writing poetry or literature that has a spiritually uplifting quality. Since Blue is your first Color, you sincerely seek to nurture others, first and foremost. Your second Color, Green, makes you want to do things in new and original ways - often, ways that you invent. With the strong need to help others, along with the need for independence, you may find yourself resisting falling into the trap of being all things to all people. In so doing, you may become fearful of being taken advantage of, or being misunderstood. Since your imagination is so powerful, you may sometimes have to force yourself (or be forced by circumstances) to see the world and other people at face value, without the overlay of your imagination. In order to provide an outlet for your imagination and intellect, it's best to find a creative outlet, where you can express the mighty inner workings of your gifted mind and heart.

As a Blue/Green/Gold/Orange, you tend to help others in both creative and orderly ways, where you know how things will turn out. Your farsightedness and ability to plan ahead enables you to spend your time wisely for the benefit of both others and yourself, just as an expert chef follows an innovative recipe and enjoys the meal, too. In a helping or healing capacity, you're almost always able to provide a sense of warm enthusiasm and composed serenity, simultaneously—which is a very rare social gift. With Orange as your last Color, you may not leap into opportunities that seem risky; in these sorts of situations, trust your intuition and inventiveness a little more. As a spiritual person, you know that opportunities don't come by accident, and your careful and discerning nature will prevail, if you do choose to take some new direction.

Your lively, can-do, helpful nature is
bolstered by your creativity.

Whether others know it or not, you are the one who is
making sure that people are getting done what needs to get
done, while getting cared for in the ways they need to be cared
for. The reason that others may not know this is that you're
not likely to blow your own horn. It's only when people take
the time to consider who or what is really maintaining so
much detailed order and solid effectiveness in the everyday
running of things, that they realize that it's you, holding things
and people together. You do this because you have the caring,

© Erica W. Lowry & Don Lowry, 2014. www.donlowry.com

"Blue glue" to accomplish that, while your work ethic is solid Gold. Once people recognize this truth about you, they find you invaluable.

With Blue as your first Color, you do like to socialize, but with Gold as your second Color, you do so only after all the work is done. (It's best if your work includes talking to others!) So when it's time to socialize, you do that with both orderliness, and a warm human touch. This makes you a wonderful host or hostess for traditional celebrations. In fact, in doing anything that involves planning, where people are concerned—you shine. You tend to help keep everyone around you better-organized, through daily acts of thoughtfulness and concern. When others show their appreciation, you rightly enjoy it, although you rarely, if ever, ask for it.

As a Blue/Gold/Orange/Green, you're hands-on, efficient, energetic, and at times highly creative. You enjoy making things run smoothly, especially in ways that can make life a bit more fun. You're a good team player; you provide the organization necessary for people to be healthy, effective, and happy. You're not likely to hem and haw about your decisions; you're a "do it now" sort of person, who has a lot of ingenuity in a pinch. And yet, you have the practicality to make wise decisions, and help others do the same. Just remember to remain open to new ideas that come your way. Your pale Green can sometimes prevent you from seeing the benefit of a completely new or abstract perspective, which ultimately may prove helpful.

You are Blue/Orange/Gold/Green . . .

You can foresee and organize the best
ways for people to grow, learn, and enjoy
themselves.

With Blue as your Primary Color, you need to create harmony and help others. This is motivated by your Orange desire to help people have fun - and also to have fun, yourself. You have the unusual ability to bring out people's child-like side, which is innocent, vulnerable, and open to anything. In your relationships with others, you're like the icing on the cake—your specialty is to help people be happier and enjoy themselves, through the many thoughtful, fun and creative things you love to do. You spend considerable effort coming up with things for people to look forward to, enjoy, and benefit from. For most, this would be a titanic effort—but not for you. It's something you do naturally.

Being Blue first, you're likely to be drawn to a helping profession, but with a second Orange you also need to be in a high energy situation where troubleshooting, creative self-expression, and a good sense of humor come into play. In anything you do, you bring a caring, human touch—and you'll also contribute the playful, creative energy of a child. Trouble enters when people think that because you're such a people-person, that you can't be hurt, which you can be, deeply— due to your very sensitive Blue side. And sometimes, you are caught between your Blue desire to be nurturing to others, and your Orange desire to be center-stage.

As a Blue/Orange/Gold/Green, you excel at ideating and organizing ways to help people have more meaningful, fun lives. You may be content not to take the #1 center-stage position in what you do, but instead work behind the scenes. The details are important to you, and you know that if they're not looked after, that plans go awry. Just be sure that you've been open to looking at all the different angles and ideas that a situation might present; being pale Green signifies that you may sometimes overlook some new ways of doing things.

You are Blue/Green/Orange/Gold . . .

You have the soul of a poet - you are sensitive, perceptive, creative, and astute.

Your strong desire to help others is achieved through your sensitive, original approach. You are deeply imaginative, and you enjoy creating new ways to be of service to others, in whatever position you find yourself. You enjoy sharing your helpful, unique creations. In fact, you most enjoy helping others through communication: writing, talking, or artistic expression. And you probably enjoy reading or writing poetry or literature that has a spiritually uplifting quality.

© Erica W. Lowry & Don Lowry, 2014. www.donlowry.com

Since Blue is your first Color, you sincerely seek to nurture others, first and foremost. Your second Color, Green, makes you want to do things in your own fashion. With the strong need to help others, along with the need for independence, you may find yourself resisting falling into the trap of being all things to all people. In so doing, you may become fearful of being taken advantage of, or getting hurt. Since your imagination is so powerful, you may sometimes have to force yourself (or be forced by circumstances) to see the world and other people at face value, without the overlay of your imagination. In order to provide an outlet for your imagination and intellect, it's best to find a creative outlet, where you can express the mighty inner workings of your gifted mind and heart.

As a Blue/Green/Orange/Gold, your drive to be creative is even stronger, as is your need to take risks, accomplish big things, and gain the recognition of others. These are Orange traits that influence you. This puts you in the position of needing lots of time with others, and also lots of time alone, since the more private Color, Green, is your second Color. As a pale Gold, the need for balance in your life won't be top priority; so in order to keep your social life and your inner life healthy, be sure to schedule your time so that you can get enough of both—but not too much of either. You may get too pulled into group activity, or too pulled into solitary activity, if you're not mindful of this tendency. In a state of outer/inner balance, you can accomplish unusually original, creative feats that will help many people.

© Erica W. Lowry & Don Lowry, 2014. www.donlowry.com

Orange

 FLEXIBLE

 DECISIVE

 PRACTICAL

 ADVENTUROUS

How I See Myself

I see life as an adventure, where I am leading the way. I live in the moment, in the here and now. So I don't hesitate to act. When I face difficulties, I see them as opportunities—I count on my resourcefulness, my sense of humor, my hands-on dexterity, and my communication skills to get through just about anything. Some may see my spontaneity as impulsiveness, but I have faith in my own abilities, and the way I see it, if it's worth doing, it's worth doing now.

What goes along with my spontaneity is an ability to make results-oriented decisions quickly. I know how to trouble-shoot, and negotiate my way through all manner of situations. In negotiation, one of the strengths I have at my disposal is my sense of humor. No matter what's going on, I'm able to make people laugh, and lighten the moment. I can find humor in just about everything—and I never take myself too seriously. In negotiation, this helps with gaining a new perspective, preventing conflict, and developing trust.

My sense of humor and adventure motivates people. I can make things fun. And I don't hesitate to show enthusiastic support of others. People that work with me like the way I create a stimulating atmosphere, and keep everyone motivated as part of a team. I think that motivation and teamwork are the first keys to getting anything done.

I'm also very hands-on, and love to be engaged in a variety of tasks. I like to be at the center of things, doing something that gets a clear, quick result. I'm project-oriented, because projects give me the results I'm looking for. I like to be the leader of the team that wins. My competitive spirit, and my "can-do" nature get things done, especially when I can get my hands dirty. (I can also fix just just about anything.) Not much stands in they way of my moving forward.

"Possibility" is my middle name. To me, life is all about new possibilities—seeing them, and making them real and tangible. I don't need to deeply analyze what we need to do. What I do is act boldly, based on clear goals.

"Be ready to be direct, spontaneous, and to have some fun."

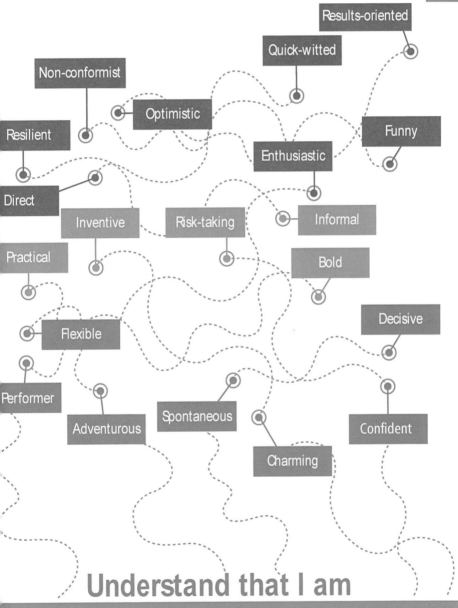

Results-oriented

Quick-witted

Non-conformist

Optimistic

Funny

Resilient

Enthusiastic

Direct

Inventive

Risk-taking

Informal

Practical

Bold

Decisive

Flexible

Performer

Spontaneous

Confident

Adventurous

Charming

Understand that I am

most positive, when you acknowledge and support how I see myself.

The Color Guide to Life
© Erica W. Lowry & Don Lowry, 2014. www.donlowry.com

What it means to be ORANGE

▶ I like to think about possibilities, options, and how to get things done. I also like to think about fun things to do. But I much prefer to do them, rather than think about them.

▶ The best way to engage me is to ask me to do something new, to get the best results. Whatever it is, I will figure it out.

▶ I will continue to be an active participant if you maintain your sense of humor, and give me the freedom to perform in my own fashion.

▶ I am least likely to respond to negative attitudes. I am a "can-do" person.

▶ You will lose my attention if you talk and talk and talk, with no action being taken.

▶ I want relationships that give me the freedom to be myself—spontaneous and adventurous.

▶ I naturally sustain and promote individuality and freedom.

▶ Things I don't enjoy are spending a lot of time doing nothing, or doing things that don't get clear or quick results.

▶ My ideal role is to be engaged in taking decisive action toward a clear goal.

▶ I feel strongest about myself when I get big, positive, immediate results from my actions.

© Erica W. Lowry & Don Lowry, 2014. www.donlowry.com

▶ **My greatest everyday stress** occurs when I feel controlled or held back by others, or when the tools I use don't work.

▶ **If I am stressed, or in a bad mood, you need to:** Give me the opportunity to play, compete, or do something physical . . . or make me laugh, to help me feel more like myself.

▶ **My greatest fear is** to have no ability to act, when I need to.

▶ **I like my spiritual life to be** fun, stimulating, powerfully moving, even physical.

▶ **In a love relationship, I tend to** seek a passionate, vibrant, fun partner, who appreciates my spontaneity.

"What I do is act boldly, based on clear goals."

The best way to engage me is by . . .

▶ Asking me to solve a problem

▶ Seeking out my resourcefulness, my dexterity, and my physical skill

▶ Respecting my "can-do" attitude and encouraging me to do things my way

▶ Enjoying my sense of humor, and sharing yours

▶ Praising my quick results, and rewarding my results

"I am most content, when I am testing my own limits - and getting the results I want."

I function best in an environment where:

▶ I feel free to be who I am

▶ I can make a real impact with my actions

▶ I feel celebrated for my decisiveness, my actions, and my sense of humor

▶ There is plenty of room for movement

▶ I can listen to music

▶ People are in a good mood

▶ There is plenty of variety in my tasks

▶ People can make noise

▶ Tools work efficiently

"I function best in environment where people can make noise."

What's My Change Style?

The pace of change has accelerated, and shows no sign of slowing down. "Disruption" of existing industries, and higher expectations to continually innovate and adapt, have become the norm. Whether or not you take an active role in creating change yourself, we all participate in the new normal. So it's key to have an understanding of change. It happens in stages, and different kinds of people with very different strengths are needed at every stage, in order for change to succeed and be sustained.

You have an optimal, essential role. What are Oranges' natural strengths, in each stage of enacting change?

In conceiving of the need for change . . .

Oranges live to **instigate** change; they **motivate** the desire for it, and **demonstrate** the possible outcomes of any changes needed.

In developing change concepts . . .

Oranges are **mobilizing** others to change, already **optimizing** the possible outcomes of change – or attempting to—and they're already **doing** the things that are being envisioned, within any change.

In finalizing change concepts . . .

Oranges leap forward, and are **building upon the changes** that others seek to implement—they are **playing** within the new structures or parameters, **testing** out the limits—and they are already **selling** whatever ideas, practices, or products need to be sold or conveyed to others.

In enacting change . . .

Oranges are already **performing, closing, and seeking to deliver**, as though any planned-for change has already occurred.

Communicating with Me

Remember: As an Orange, I like action-words.

Your Ideal Approach: Be ready to be direct and spontaneous and to have some fun.

Your Ideal Tone: Light-hearted, friendly, relaxed, willing to joke.

Your Ideal Topics: What to do, in the present or immediate future.

Your Ideal Openers - Active and Concrete:

▶ "I want to know what you want, and I'll tell you what I can do, to help you get it."

▶ "Here's what I want to do with you: _____
_____ "

▶ "You're a trouble-shooter. Can you help me with this?"

▶ "Let's get this business over and done with, so that we can go on to more exciting topics."

▶ "Can you use your magic sauce, to get this done?"

Your Ideal Rebuttals - Direct and Concrete:

▶ "I disagree. I think that . . ."

▶ "I don't see that. Tell me what I'm missing."

▶ 'That's a problem. How can we solve it?"

▶ "I think you're wrong, there. How do you see that?"

© Erica W. Lowry & Don Lowry, 2014. www.donlowry.com

▶ "Wow! That's amazing! YOU are AMAZING!!!"

▶ "Ha ha ha ha ha ha, ha ha ha ha ha ha, ha ha ha . . . (Oh no, I think I just peed.)"

▶ "You totally aced that presentation! High five!"

▶ " . . . Wait, that's awesome. Let me put that on Twitter."

Your Ideal Humor: Orange people find humor in anything, anywhere—so any humor is always welcome, even if it's not that funny. An Orange person can turn any joke you make into a funnier joke.

Never, Ever: Try to force an Orange person to do something that he or she feels is very boring, or which has little or no impact . . . at least not more than once. (Unless, that is, you have a very compelling "carrot.") Never treat an Orange person like they're not being useful when they're trying to be useful, or not as skilled as they like to be, when their skillfulness is called for—or like they're ever, in any way, boring. . . . But you probably won't have occasion to suggest any of those things.

> "You will lose my attention if you talk and talk and talk, with no action being taken."

What I have in Common WITH OTHER COLORS

Like Blues,
I am very creative, enthusiastic, and generous.

Like Greens,
I love change and variety, and I am easily bored.

Like Golds,
I am very concrete, and I appreciate rules that make perfect sense.

© Erica W. Lowry & Don Lowry, 2014. www.donlowry.com

My Health and Wellness

In Order to be Healthy, my own needs and values must be incorporated into any health and wellness process. I also need to be able to use my personal strengths, in becoming and staying healthy. As an ORANGE, any health and wellness program I engage in has to be FUN and EXCITING in some way, or I won't stay with it. I'll be successful in a health and wellness process if I know I can count on:

▶ Getting fairly quick, obvious results

▶ Having fun, getting lots of positive feedback

▶ Plenty of variety, changes in scenery

▶ Enjoying competition, games - and winning

▶ Improving my physical skills and dexterity

I need to be aware of:

▶ The fact that I may seek fun & excitement through fun snacks and fast food, whenever life isn't fun and exciting enough

▶ The fact that the quick, obvious results I seek may take a little while, but the immediate result will be having a good time, and knowing that results are coming

▶ The fact that I need to engage in activities that challenge my skill and dexterity, not just my strength and endurance

▶ My tendency to overdo it—with repetitions, with taking risks, and with energy-boosting sports drinks

I consider my health and wellness to be:

▶ Something I don't take too seriously, but still a big part of who I am

▶ Something that should come naturally

© Erica W. Lowry & Don Lowry, 2014. www.donlowry.com

92 I prefer to learn about health information by:

▶ Being told about it when I need to learn something

▶ Surfing the Internet

What will motivate me to improve my health and wellness is:

▶ A program where a TOP PRIORITY is having fun

▶ Knowing that my results will be obvious

▶ Knowing that it will not be complex, but simple and easy

▶ Not having to deprive myself of foods I love

▶ Feeling like it's something I will just naturally want to do

"For me, it has to be fun."

'I consider my health to be something
that should come naturally."

93

My Primary Causes of Stress

▶ Feeling that I don't make a clear impact, with what I do

▶ Feeling controlled by others

▶ Work that is too routine and boring

▶ Not being able to express my sense of humor

▶ Not having money to spend

▶ Being "all work and no play"

▶ Not being "stroked" enough

▶ No opportunity to compete

▶ Being forced to work alone in a cramped environment

When I am stressed, I tend to . . .

▶ Act impulsively

▶ Become angry, even belligerent at times

▶ Make cutting remarks

▶ Accidentally hurt myself

▶ Slam doors and yell

Please Don't:

▶ Talk and talk and talk, when something needs to get done

▶ Ignore my sense of humor

- ▶ Give me too many tasks that are routine and boring
- ▶ Restrict my creativity
- ▶ Expect me to follow policies that don't make sense
- ▶ Ask me to attend meeting after meeting, where I sit for hours
- ▶ Mess with my tools (whether it be a drill bit, a drum-set, or a hard drive)
- ▶ Insult my performance, publicly

"Please don't restrict my creativity."

▶ When obstacles arise, it's best that I look for the humor in a situation, while I figure out what to do. It immediately puts things in perspective, for me and everyone else. This is one of my greatest gifts: I need to use it.

▶ I love a sense of freedom, and I have a natural, kinetic charm. So if I'm restless or feeling stuck, I keep something with me to remind me of my playful nature. Not a phone that I'll stare into, but say, a little whirligig on my keychain. A finger-puzzle. A toy. Literally, a kinetic charm on a chain. My harmless playing keeps me centered on the people and the discussion at hand.

▶ Rule of thumb: Never tease a Blue person, with what I think is "affectionate teasing." It always backfires. It's a bad idea.

▶ I tend to overload on tasks, because I'm an optimist. But I'm also very concrete. I can take up the Gold concrete habit, of making to-do lists. Lists tend to be boring, so I can make them fun by adding REWARDS associated with each task I complete (i.e., "Submitting Expense Report = Movie night w/popcorn.") Everyone will LOVE that I keep lists, and I'll love reaping all the rewards.

▶ As an Orange, everyone knows that I like to keep my options open, that I like my freedom, and that I like to make a big impact. But it's best if I express to others the commitments that I have, through lots of little concrete actions that I take. . . . They build solid trust.

▶ In order to be happy I need to surround myself with possibility, all manner of color, things that move, things that make noise, people who laugh at my jokes, opportunities for winning—and celebration—and tools that work.

There are 24 possible variations of True Colors Spectrum. Which one are you?

You are Orange/Blue/Gold/Green . . .

> You enrich everyone's life through your understanding of what people really want and need.

Your Orange strengths for creating fun and adventure are motivated through your Blue need to help and nurture others. You truly are the go-to person, if groups of people or individuals want to enjoy themselves, feel fulfilled, and feel supported. Your upbeat, enthusiastic, social and trouble-shooting nature allows you to easily deal with any issue that involves other people—with groups, or where personalized attention is required. You take quick action with genuine care, in both social and personal issues. While others may shy away from dealing with dozens (or even thousands) of interpersonal interactions and issues at once, you thrive in this area.

You are highly creative by nature; it may be in music, visual art, creative writing, or in anything else you do. At work, you are naturally talented in creating more personal, fun forms of doing business. You need the freedom to be creative, and must have enjoyable relationships where you help others feel good. It's best if you can include these talents both at work and at home. (However, since everyone notices your nimble social gifts and your helpful nature, people will be eager to put these talents to use.) You may sometimes notice that your need to be center-stage, and your need to nurture others, come into conflict in yourself. Best to be center-stage while helping others—because you excel at doing just that.

As an Orange/Blue/Gold/Green, you're likely to take risks like any Orange person, but you'll do it wisely, with planning. Your enthusiastic, helpful nature is tinged with the need to be useful in very practical ways. Your Gold enhances your Blue, in making you a very caring person in many responsible ways —and your Gold enhances your Orange, in that you like to help others have fun in ways that are concrete and everyday, rather than abstract. You're willing to be very orderly, if need be; with your highly social nature, people might not expect that added bonus. With a pale Green, you'll just need to remember that some people are not nearly as communicative as you, and delays in communication are not necessarily a reflection of their feelings about you.

> You hold the map that leads to change; you yourself, are that route.

IMPOSSIBLE

Your Orange strengths for creating more excitement and adventure in life are motivated through your Green needs to innovate and improve the world. Your spontaneous, hands-on ingenuity is rare in trouble-shooting situations; you can be counted on for more than just the occasional stroke of genius. In addition, your quick, original sense of humor is central to your personality. This sense of humor, of course, is a symptom of a keen intelligence. You see change happening before it happens—often, because you're the one making it happen.

The Color Guide to Life
© Erica W. Lowry & Don Lowry, 2014. www.donlowry.com

You're likely to lead others, which brings group exploration and invention to a whole new level.

With fun-loving Orange as your first Color, and curious Green as your second, you're one of those that others marvel at, but don't often understand. Your willingness to experiment on a large scale is really extraordinary. You're willing to make the occasional mistake, in order to learn something new, and then immediately move on. This playful, concrete ideation is an inspiration to others, and it helps forward-movement in a tangible way. You may sometimes experience an inner-conflict between your Orange need to take adventurous risks, and your Green, perfectionistic need to always be competent.

As an Orange/Green/Gold/Blue, you're likely to be entrepreneurial, or a person who leads in innovation. You're likely to manage your risks wisely. You're a strong personality that others are drawn to, because while being inventive, funny, and ingenious, you're also well-organized. Thus, you'll probably be successful in your endeavors. Just remember that the assistance of others is key to your long-term success. If you remember to fully acknowledge the help of others, you're likely to get where you're going—which is probably an ambitious position that spans a wide variety of responsibilities. At work and at home, be sure to remember that family members and friends need affirmations of your feelings.

You are Orange/Gold/Blue/Green . . .

Your amazing task-mastery serves the good of others.

Your Orange strengths for doing things quickly and well are motivated through your Gold need to get concrete results. You're very hands-on, in getting things done right. Being Orange first, trouble-shooting new problems is also an area of expertise, and for you it's a practical, fun thing to do, even in an emergency. In a leadership capacity you can provide the motivation, the flexibility, and the structure to accomplish a vast quantity of big and small tasks—including physical tasks. You love hard work, working hard with others, and you do enjoy the reward.

© Erica W. Lowry & Don Lowry, 2014. www.donlowry.com

You are action-oriented, and respectful of rules that make sense. While you want to have fun, much of your enjoyment comes from personal accomplishment and gaining well-earned recognition (and pay). Your natural respect for sensible rules and your financial foresight provide a sense of security, in work and at home. But you also know that real reward includes real fun—as in, socializing. You like to let go of your Gold side occasionally, and really have a fantastic, adventurous time. You love to laugh. If you ever have any inner-conflicts (which would be rare), they're between your need to have fun, and your need to follow the rules.

As an Orange/Gold/Blue/Green, you use your task-mastery and troubleshooting abilities mainly to help others. You have a friendly, welcoming side that facilitates others' cooperation, making it possible for you to manage many projects where people are concerned. Your Blue enhances your Gold, making you an extremely honest, caring person, and your Blue enhances your Orange, making you more generous and creative. Your pale Green sometimes prevents you from seeing the advantage of new or abstract ideas; you're focused on getting things done the way you know they should be done, which you know works for you and others. Try to remain open to abstract alternatives, because sometimes even very abstract ideas can be utilized in ways that get concrete results.

You love living life to the fullest - which for you, means helping others to do that, too.

Your Orange strengths for creating fun and adventure are motivated through your Blue need to help and nurture others. You truly are the go-to person, if groups of people or individuals want to enjoy themselves, feel fulfilled, and feel supported. Your upbeat, enthusiastic, social and trouble-shooting nature allows you to easily deal with any issue that involves other people—with groups, or where personalized attention is required. You take quick action with genuine care, in both social and personal issues. While others may shy away

© Erica W. Lowry & Don Lowry, 2014. www.donlowry.com

from dealing with dozens (or even thousands) of interpersonal interactions and issues at once, you thrive in this area.

You are highly creative by nature; it may be in music, visual art, creative writing, or in anything else you do. At work, you are naturally talented in creating more personal, fun forms of doing business. You need the freedom to be creative, and must have enjoyable relationships where you help others feel good. It's best if you can include these talents both at work and at home. (However, since everyone notices your nimble social gifts and your helpful nature, people will be eager to put these talents to use.) You may sometimes notice that your need to be center-stage, and your need to nurture others, come into conflict in yourself. Best to be center-stage while helping others—because you excel at doing just that.

As an Orange/Blue/Green/Gold, you're an idea-factory for creating and implementing ways to help people enjoy themselves, while also enriching the meaning of people's lives. Your Green enhances your Blue and Orange, in creative ideation—that is, in coming up with wondrous, brand new ideas; and your Green enhances your Orange, in creating change, whether personal or social. Despite your social nature, you're also likely to want to handle many tasks by yourself; your strong Green makes you independent. With a pale Gold, just be sure that you've got the details of projects well-taken care of, in advance. Your enthusiastic, can-do, innovative nature ensures that you'll leap on interesting opportunities.

> You live life out on a limb — but as they say,
> that's where the fruit is.

Your Orange strengths for creating more excitement and adventure in life are motivated through your Green needs to innovate and improve the world. Your spontaneous, hands-on ingenuity is rare in trouble-shooting situations; you can be counted on for more than just the occasional stroke of genius. In addition, your quick, original sense of humor is central to your personality. This sense of humor, of course, is a symptom of a keen intelligence. You see change happening before it happens, often because you're the one making it happen.

© Erica W. Lowry & Don Lowry, 2014. www.donlowry.com

You're likely to lead others, which brings group exploration and invention to a whole new level.

With fun-loving Orange as your first Color, and curious Green as your second, you're one of those that others marvel at, but don't often understand. Your willingness to experiment on a large scale is really extraordinary. You're willing to make the occasional mistake, in order to learn something new—and then immediately move on. This playful, concrete ideation is an inspiration to others, and it helps forward-movement in a tangible way. You may sometimes experience an inner-conflict between your Orange need to take genuine risks, and your Green, perfectionistic need to be ever-competent.

As an Orange/Green/Blue/Gold, you're likely to want to use your strengths to help others, through new and original ways (probably, your own way). Others appreciate your ability to encourage and include others, while you're innovating. You have a poetic streak; you're probably a lover of great literature, music, and art. You may be an artist, yourself. And you love a good laugh; you're the rare soul whom others are likely to anoint as "wacky." With Gold last, try to be careful in planning ahead, in your many ongoing projects. Try to get the help of those who are brighter Gold to assist you, and/or work to strengthen your own long-term planning abilities. If you can improve your ability to plan ahead, the potential for your success can be enormous.

You're the expert in getting solid results.

Your Orange strengths for doing things quickly and well are motivated through your Gold need to get concrete results. You're very hands-on, in getting things done right. Being Orange first, troubleshooting new problems is also an area of expertise, and for you it's a practical, fun thing to do, even in an emergency. In a leadership capacity you can provide the motivation, the flexibility, and the structure to accomplish a vast quantity of big and small tasks—including physical tasks. You love hard work, working hard with others, and you do enjoy the reward.

© Erica W. Lowry & Don Lowry, 2014. www.donlowry.com

You are action-oriented, and respectful of rules that make sense. While you want to have fun, much of your enjoyment comes from personal accomplishment and gaining well-earned recognition (and pay). Your natural respect for sensible rules and your financial foresight provide a sense of security, in work and at home. But you also know that real reward includes real fun—as in, socializing. You like to let go of your Gold side occasionally, and really have a fantastic, adventurous time. You love to laugh. If you ever have any inner-conflicts (which would be rare), they're between your need to have fun, and your need to follow the rules.

As an Orange/Gold/Green/Blue, you come up with great ideas for creating new ways for getting things done. You're an idea factory for new ways to accomplish tasks in concrete ways. Your Green enhances your Gold, making you highly strategic and logical. Your Green enhances your Orange, in that you are willing to take some chances with innovation and invention, if they are wise investments of time and money. Your Green also enhances your Orange, in making you more of a big-picture person. Your pale Blue signifies that you could pay a bit more attention to the need to acknowledge others' feelings. If acknowledged, people are more willing to see the advantages of your useful ways for getting things done.

© Erica W. Lowry & Don Lowry, 2014. www.donlowry.com

Gold

 DEPENDABLE

 ORGANIZED

 LOYAL

 TRUSTWORTHY

I would describe myself as solid as a rock. I like to stay grounded in reality. I am most comfortable when I have clear guidelines concerning how I should live my life, what I should do, and when. That way, there are no surprises. I have a strong desire to conform to what is expected of me, so that I don't cause any unnecessary stress. I like to stay grounded within the established structures of our society, so that everyone is safe and secure. I do these things, because I sincerely care about my community, my country, my family, and the organizations I serve.

I lead a life that is well-organized, dependable, hard-working, honest and loyal. It's clear to me that responsibility and usefulness are the practical underpinnings of any successful enterprise, be it a company, a school, or a family. I also use my time intelligently, to do all that I can to promote and model the work-ethic that I feel serves everyone best.

But that doesn't mean I don't hope that others will help out, too. They say, "the devil is in the details," because the details are the hard work. I like it when everyone has an eye on making sure the details are properly taken care of, because that ensures that a stable foundation will be well established, for everyone's success.

Some people may think that I'm not as fun-loving a person as others, but that's not true. I enjoy having fun just as much as the next person. But I need to know that things are properly taken care of, before I feel that it's time to have some well-earned fun. I see that as the caring and reasonable

© Erica W. Lowry & Don Lowry, 2014. www.donlowry.com

approach. I particularly enjoy traditional celebrations that my family has always celebrated. This reminds me of what is most important to me: family, mutual caring and respect, stability, and following age-old cherished traditions.

I do enjoy progress, like most people. But progress requires a strong foundation, a solid plan, hard work, and steady discipline. I am someone who can be counted on, to ensure that every step along the way is steadfastly adhered to, every day. On a daily basis, in any organization, I am the strongest link in the chain.

> **"I am most comfortable when I have clear guidelines concerning how I should live my life, what I should do, and when."**

"I particularly enjoy traditional celebrations that my family has always celebrated."

© Erica W. Lowry & Don Lowry, 2014. www.donlowry.com

Caring	Ethical	Patient	Steady
Committed	Helpful	Precise	Trustworthy
Conservative	Honest	Predictable	Useful
Consistent	Loyal	Punctual	
Cooperative	Orderly	Responsible	
Dependable	Organized		
Detail-oriented			
Diligent			

Understand that I am

most positive, when you acknowledge and support how I see myself.

What it means to be GOLD

▶ I like to think about my thorough plans, which I will accomplish in an organized fashion, in order to do what I have set out to do.

▶ My ideal role is to plan ahead, and maintain a clear, step-by-step course of action.

▶ The best way to engage me is to be helpful in maintaining procedure. If you see that I am busy, which I probably am, please do not interrupt without first politely asking me for my time. I will always do the same for you.

▶ I will continue to be an active participant if you stay on-task and cooperative, with any matter at hand.

▶ I am least likely to respond to abstract ideas that don't adhere to a plan, or what I consider to be ill-mannered behavior such as interrupting, unruliness, or being tardy.

▶ I want relationships that are dignified, dependable, and cooperative.

▶ I am most excited about completing tasks thoroughly, on-time, and according to plan.

▶ I naturally sustain and promote dutifulness and responsibility.

▶ You will lose my attention if you are too abstract. Please be clear and concrete.

▶ Things I don't enjoy are sudden surprises that disturb an established plan or status quo.

© Erica W. Lowry & Don Lowry, 2014. www.donlowry.com

► I feel strongest about myself when everyone works together like a well-oiled machine, because I am doing my job of maintaining order successfully.

► My greatest everyday stress occurs when others do not follow policies, when they break promises, don't follow through, and when I take on too much work because others do not handle the details well.

► If I am stressed, or in a bad mood, you need to: Give me time, space, and quiet, and offer to help me with the tasks at hand.

► I like my spiritual life to be traditional, with a community of people that I know and respect.

► In a love relationship, I tend to seek a partner who is respectful, and who will help me to uphold the traditional values of home and family.

"I naturally sustain and promote dutifullness and responsibility."

The best way to engage me is by:

▶ Being polite and respectful

▶ Discussing what needs to be done and how to do it

▶ Being clear and concrete

▶ Respecting my time and abilities

▶ Following through - on time

"I want relationships that are dignified, dependable, and cooperative."

I function best in an environment where:

▶ Expectations are clearly defined

▶ Everyone fully understands protocol, and follows it

▶ People are respectful of others' time and privacy

▶ There are realistic considerations given to budgetary and time constraints

▶ I can easily bring closure to tasks in a timely manner

▶ I have private space to work

▶ It is quiet, with few interruptions

▶ There is very little or no chaos

▶ I feel valued for my loyalty, responsibility, and organizational abilities

▶ People do not bring their personal problems to work

▶ Others are good at follow-through with me, so that we can stay on schedule

"Please don't keep me waiting."

The Color Guide to Life
© Erica W. Lowry & Don Lowry, 2014. www.donlowry.com

What's My Change Style?

The pace of change has accelerated, and shows no sign of slowing down. "Disruption" of existing industries, and higher expectations to continually innovate and adapt, have become the norm. Whether or not you take an active role in creating change yourself, we all participate in the new normal. So it's key to have an understanding of change. It happens in stages, and different kinds of people with very different strengths are needed at every stage, in order for change to succeed and be sustained.

You have an optimal, essential role. What are Golds' natural strengths, in each stage of creating change?

In conceiving of the need for change . . .

Golds play the critical role of **reviewing** ideas and input, **prioritizing** them, and **scheduling** tasks so that ideas and influences are mapped out and carefully integrated by all parties involved.

In developing change concepts . . .

Golds play the role of **economizing** at the outset, **risk-assessing** very carefully, and **planning** for any possible future contingencies and expenses.

In finalizing change concepts . . .

Golds will carefully **evaluate** for errors, provide methods to **rectify**, and give knowledgeable **warning** of possible future pitfalls.

In enacting change . . .

Golds play the crucial role of **managing** the practices of any changes enacted; they will continue to **scrutinize** results, and they will work to **fool-proof** any new changes that have been put in place, to make certain that they are successful.

© Erica W. Lowry & Don Lowry, 2014. www.donlowry.com

"I am most content, when everything goes exactly as planned."

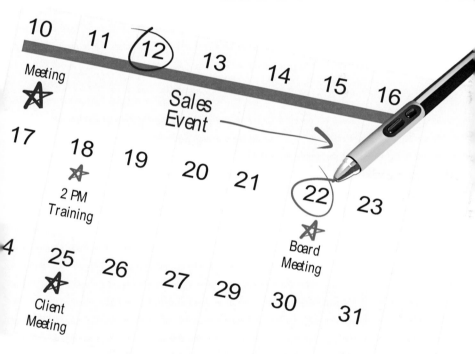

Communicating with Me

Remember: Never rush through information, and always be well-prepared.

Your Ideal Approach: To assist through step-by-step, clear, achievable goals.

Your Ideal Tone: Friendly but formal, polite, appropriate and efficient.

Your Ideal Topics: What ought to be done, and precisely how.

Your Ideal Openers - Polite and Respectful:

▶ "I know you're very busy - when do you have some time? I need twenty minutes, to discuss . . ."

▶ "I want to talk about what achievable goals we can set for _____, and the steps to take, to meet those goals."

▶ "I've prepared an outline for us to review. It will take about ___ minutes."

▶ "Let's find out what we need to do, to keep this problem from repeating itself. When do you have ___ minutes?"

Your Ideal Rebuttals - Respectful, Step-by-Step and Goal-Oriented:

▶ "I see how that makes sense. But I think our long-term goal of _____ may be even more achievable if we . . ."

▶ "I see. However if you look at this situation with other certain facts in mind, such as _____, maybe you'll see that . . ."

© Erica W. Lowry & Don Lowry, 2014. www.donlowry.com

> "I can see your point. But I need some time to consider your thoughts, in order to come to you with a plan that I can share, and get your opinions."

> "I'll let you know by . . ."

> "That's a good step to take. But I think it might be even more helpful to you, if . . ."

Your Ideal Praise - Very Specific, Well-Earned, and Showing Results:

> "Your work created a 39% increase in participation, which created a 12% increase in profits over last quarter."

> "Your family must be so proud of you, for . . . (specific thing)"

> "Our talks together always feel like time well spent. I learned from you, that . . . (state specific thing, & its benefit)."

> "I appreciate it that you help me do my job so well. It makes my life easier. For instance . . . (state specific thing that saves time)."

> "You really showed dedication. That was admirable. It made all the difference, because . . . (state specific benefit that happened)."

Your Ideal Humor: Gold people are generally amused by the disarray of others in life, and the chaos in life situations. They also enjoy witty, wry, light sarcasm that helps them keep their good nature and objectivity.

Never, Ever: Make a Gold person feel ill-prepared or disorganized, or criticize them for being late. If they're late they know it only too well.

The Color Guide to Life
© Erica W. Lowry & Don Lowry, 2014. www.donlowry.com

"Fairness and the rule of law are the cornerstone of any successful society."

The Color Guide to Life
© Erica W. Lowry & Don Lowry, 2014. www.donlowry.com

What I have in Common WITH OTHER COLORS

Like Blues,
I am committed to the service of others, I value cooperation, and I work to uphold family traditions.

Like Greens,
I pay attention to detail, I value my privacy, I enjoy doing research when necessary, and it's important to me that things stay under control.

Like Oranges,
I am very concrete, and I appreciate good rules.

The Color Guide to Life
© Erica W. Lowry & Don Lowry, 2014. www.donlowry.com

My Health and Wellness

In Order to be Healthy, my own values and needs must be incorporated into any health and wellness plan. I also need to be able to use my personal strengths, in becoming and staying healthy. As a GOLD, any health and wellness program I engage in has to be EFFICIENT, THOROUGH, and MEDICALLY APPROVED, or I won't stay with it. I'll be successful in a health and wellness plan when I know that I can count on:

▶ Having a health and wellness plan that comes from a credible source, that I trust

▶ Being able to easily make time for this plan in my schedule; it must be an expedient program

▶ Having guidelines for diet and exercise that are clear, easy, step-by-step, and inexpensive, with expected outcomes clearly stated

▶ Knowing that my program is medically approved for someone of my gender, weight, and age

▶ Having easy access to all of the information I need, very clearly presented

▶ Trusting that the person(s) supervising me behave in a dignified, respectful manner, and provide timely follow-up with my needs

I need to be aware of:

▶ My tendency to always find more work to do, instead of fitting a health and wellness plan into my busy schedule

▶ Being sedentary, if I don't see the practical, critical value of a diet/exercise routine; I just need to look at the plain facts, about the consequences of lack of exercise

▶ Thinking that a diet/fitness plan seems mostly to be

© Erica W. Lowry & Don Lowry, 2014. www.donlowry.com

about trying hard to look a certain way, which is not my primary life concern—I need to remember that is just about *health*, which is the most valuable thing that I can have

I consider my health and wellness to be:

▶ A personal issue that I discuss with my doctor and adult relatives

▶ An important issue, because people depend upon me

I like to learn about health information by:

▶ Reading about it in books, pamphlets and periodicals that I trust

▶ Hearing about it from qualified professionals

What will motivate me to improve my health and wellness is:

▶ A research-based, medically approved approach

▶ Clear, step-by-step guidelines with expected outcomes and proven effective results

▶ Convenience

▶ Ensuring that the program is not too time-consuming

▶ A gym that is clean, well-lit, and sanitary

▶ Supervisors who are punctual, and thorough with instruction and follow-up

My Primary Causes of Stress

▶ Chaos at work or at home

▶ Worries about money

▶ Worries about my health or the health of my loved ones

▶ Being overworked

▶ Lack of control at work or at home

▶ Others' disrespect of policies and established plans

▶ Emotional drama

▶ Conflict with my seniors at work, when they expect me to constantly change plans, or do not provide clear guidelines

▶ Others' messiness and sloppiness

When I am very stressed I tend to:

▶ Become self-righteous

▶ Shut down to others

▶ Complain

▶ Try to force others to follow rules

Please Don't:

▶ Keep me waiting

▶ Digress in conversation, when we are discussing plans and procedures

The Color Guide to Life
© Erica W. Lowry & Don Lowry, 2014. www.donlowry.com

▶ Interrupt me in my work, without politely asking to speak with me

▶ Disrespect the importance of my organizational abilities

▶ Expect me to clean up others' messes, which were made due to others' irresponsibility

▶ Change plans often, or go off-course of plan without warning

▶ Speak abstractly when issuing instructions—instead, provide clear, step-by-step instructions

▶ Openly disrespect the company or those in authority, in my presence

▶ Disrupt my set of priorities by forcing me to shift gears often

"Please don't expect me to clean up other's messes."

▶ In a world full of people, chaos is inevitable. So I can calmly anticipate it, and plan for it. (Even the military expects the chaos factor, so they not only plan for it, they have humorous jargon for it, i.e., "S.N.A.F.U.")

▶ Sometimes what seems like total chaos, may be the beginning of a positive change. And since change cannot be implemented and maintained properly without me, my patience during chaos is definitely a virtue.

▶ I work long hours, because I'm dedicated. But I need to remain just as dedicated to my own rituals for health, because time invested in my health reduces sick days and is the best long-term investment that exists for me.

▶ When others fail to maintain an orderly life, it is not ever a reflection of me. It is who they choose to be. I try not to let it affect me.

▶ When I'm stressed out, "balance" is a key word for me to remind myself of , because I am *particularly* skilled at finding, creating, and maintaining it.

▶ It helps if I add "colorized" dots to my to-do lists and appointment calendar, to remind me that:

Blues always prefer a little social conversation, warm encouragement, and kind thanks, when I am asking for their help.

Greens always appreciate hearing the big picture, different options for how to take action, and invitations to open questioning, when I'm seeking their cooperation.

Oranges always like clear instructions, with some space for creativity and fun, when I need their help.

. . . Practicing this, helps me to make everyone, myself included, more efficient.

© Erica W. Lowry & Don Lowry, 2014. www.donlowry.com

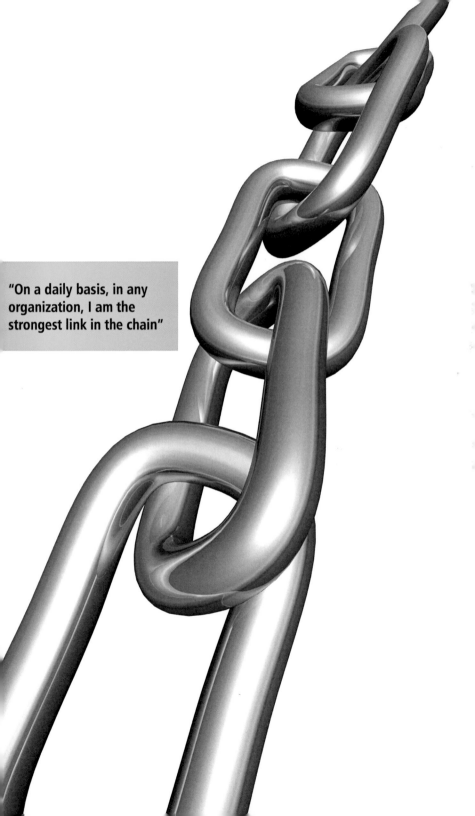

"On a daily basis, in any organization, I am the strongest link in the chain"

There are 24 possible variations of True Colors Spectrum. Which one are you?

You are Gold/Blue/Green/Orange . . .

The original saying was, "God is in the details." You embody that motto.

Your Gold strength for acting responsibly to maintain stability is motivated through your Blue need to help others. You know that people can't be supported in a long-term, tangible capacity when there's chaos, so you create the calm structure wherein help can be delivered regularly and promptly. This help is often delivered by you, personally. For you, it's a way of life to ensure stability and practical support, because this is everyone's most basic sustenance, even if they don't realize it. However, not everyone is willing to do the hard, "detail" work required to meet these foundational needs. Luckily for others, you're an expert.

You do this for one basic reason: You care. You care about others in a concrete way (as in, preventing illness or accident or chaos) and in an emotional way (as in, preventing upset). You are conscientious, honest, practical, modest, and caring to the maximal degree. You may be holding the fort down, but that may be your secret. That's okay—being Gold/Blue, your conscientiousness towards others and your spiritual dedication are so strong that you don't need many accolades from others. If you ever have any sort of inner-conflict, it's between your need to follow the rules to the letter, and your need to do things a little more creatively, sometimes.

As a Gold/Blue/Green/Orange, you're happy to work behind-the-scenes making sure that everything runs smoothly and as planned. Your third Green helps you to see ways to improve upon existing methods for doing things, and to appreciate abstract concepts. Your Green enhances your Gold in making you more logical and strategic, and your Green enhances your Blue in making you more sensitive to others' ideas. Be sure not to miss challenging new opportunities that may come your way - your pale Orange signifies that you may overlook these opportunities for yourself, in life.

You are a leader in solving problems and handling risk—but you choose your risks wisely.

Your Gold need to create stability is motivated through your Orange need to take action. You're very hands-on, so you like physical action. Physically engaged or not, you appreciate the need for physical involvement in getting things done, while following the rules. You are a disciplined person who enjoys the advantages of self-leadership, self-discipline, and active participation in assisting others. You excel at taking care of business, because you have your eye trained on both the

© Erica W. Lowry & Don Lowry, 2014. www.donlowry.com

bottom line and concrete daily activities (Gold), and on future opportunity (Orange). You're probably involved in improving your community, due to your sense of civic duty. But in any case you won't waste your time solving any problem you don't see as a realistic use of time.

While your Gold ensures that you are a person of propriety, who respects rules and those in authority, your Orange allows you to easily take charge of others, in an authority position yourself. Being second Orange, you also enjoy and excel at troubleshooting. Therefore, you are likely to end up in a leadership capacity, either directing those who perform tasks involving physical activity, while you ensure that rules are followed—or you'll do those physical tasks yourself, in a takecharge capacity. If you experience any inner-conflict, it's between your need to follow the rules to the letter, and your need to let loose and have fun.

As a Gold/Orange/Green/Blue, you possess a genius in finding practical solutions to problems involving systems and large groups of people—while also following any strict rules and regulations. Rather than dealing with individual or personal problems, you prefer tackling those big, hands-on challenges where you see a clear and highly beneficial result for many. Your third Green enhances your Gold by making you a person who is very logical and highly strategic. And your Green enhances your Orange, by making you a person who is open to quick changes of plan—you're someone who's willing to be involved in innovation, if there's a very strong, new plan. Your pale Blue signifies that you could do well to be a bit more patient with and nurturing of others, particularly those who are helping you. By recognizing their personal qualities and contributions—they'll be more helpful to you and others.

Your moral standard and your work ethic are unsurpassed.

Your Gold strength for creating stability through solid dedication is motivated through your Green need to retain, advance, and use knowledge and information correctly, for the benefit of everyone. You organize, categorize, correct, maintain and utilize appropriate information (and practices) to create the stability and durability that people and organizations require, in order to be successful. You have a strong ethical nature that ensures that you use information that is true and applicable. Your dedication to others ensures that no one will have to wait, for your clear input or proper direction. Whether your knowledge is stored in your mind, in your files, on your hard-drive, in the cloud, or on your bookshelves—others can count on you to find answers, expeditiously.

Your mind is more capable than any machine, at locating, organizing, and providing necessary, correct information and direction. You prioritize your thoughts and knowledge expertly, and you deliver individualized, detailed information and plans. You yourself lead a life that is strictly guided by the high ethical and moral standards that you set for yourself. If you ever have an occasional inner-conflict (which is rare), it's due to your need to adhere to traditional, trustworthy information and practices, and your need to create better, new information and more efficient practices.

As a Gold/Green/Blue/Orange, you use your well-informed, task-mastering abilities primarily to help others. You're drawn to organizations that assist people in tangible, concrete ways. Your third Blue enhances your Gold, by making you a person who cares about communities, schools, and organizations that do good. And your Blue enhances your Green, by making you more sensitive to others, and more reflective. This just adds positive qualities to your high personal ethic, in life. Your pale Orange signifies that you could possibly benefit by being more open to new opportunities, and that you could let your hair down, a bit more often.

You're the backbone of any organization you find yourself in.

Your Gold strength for acting responsibly to maintain stability is motivated through your Blue need to help others. You know that people can't be supported in a long-term, tangible capacity, when there's chaos—so you create the calm structure wherein help can be delivered regularly and promptly. This help is often delivered by you, personally. For you, it's a way of life to ensure stability and practical support, because this is everyone's most basic sustenance, even if they don't realize it. However, not everyone is willing to do

© Erica W. Lowry & Don Lowry, 2014. www.donlowry.com

the hard, "detail" work required to meet these foundational needs. Luckily for others, you're an expert.

You do this for one basic reason: You care. You care about others in a concrete way (as in, preventing illness, accident or chaos) and in an emotional way (as in, preventing upset). You are conscientious, honest, practical, modest, and caring to the maximal degree. You capably hold the fort down when you must, without the need of accolades. Being Gold/Blue, your conscientiousness toward others and your spiritual dedication are so strong that you don't need that many kudos from others (a simple thanks, once in a while, will do). If you ever have any sort of inner-conflict, it's between your need to follow the rules to the letter, and your need to do things a little more creatively, when you see that it's practical. You don't like to bend the rules.

As a Gold/Blue/Orange/Green, you're likely to want to help in a broad way. Your third Orange makes you want to get out there and help more people. (You also probably plan a great party for family/friends.) The reward is that you more easily allow yourself to loosen up and have some well-earned fun. Also, your third Orange enhances your Gold in making you very hands-on—and that third Orange in you "pumps up" your Blue qualities, of sociability and creativity. Your pale Green can sometimes keep you from seeing the benefit of more abstract approaches. Try to remain open to these new concepts, as they sometimes do lead to improved practices.

You take charge ably, in service to many others.

Your Gold need to create stability is motivated through your Orange need to take action. You're very hands-on, so you like physical action. Physically engaged or not, you appreciate the need for physical involvement in getting things done, while following the rules. You are a disciplined person who enjoys the advantages of self-leadership, self-discipline, and active participation in assisting others. You excel at taking care

© Erica W. Lowry & Don Lowry, 2014. www.donlowry.com

of business, because you have your eye trained on both the bottom line and concrete daily activities (Gold), and on future opportunity (Orange). You're probably involved in improving your community, due to your sense of civic duty. But in any case you won't waste your time solving any problem you don't see as a realistic use of time.

While your Gold ensures that you are a person of propriety, who respects rules and those in authority, your Orange allows you to easily take charge of others, in an authority position yourself. Being second Orange, you also enjoy and excel at troubleshooting. Therefore, you are likely to end up in a leadership capacity, either directing those who perform tasks involving physical activity, while you ensure that rules are followed—or you'll do those physical tasks yourself, in a takecharge capacity. If you experience any inner-conflict, it's between your need to follow the rules to the letter, and your need to let loose and have fun.

As a Gold/Orange/Blue/Green, you have a very strong social conscience. You want to assist organizations that do good for all. You also have a warm, welcoming quality that makes you very engaging. Others look to you not just for your sense of order and fairness and your problem-solving ability, but also for your charm and joviality. Your third Blue enhances your Gold, by making you a very sincere, caring person. And your Blue enhances your Orange, by making you more social, and more creative in your troubleshooting. You're very willing to hear out the opinions of others, but your pale Green signifies that you could benefit by being more open to abstract ideas, which may at first seem highly impractical. Be sure to remember that some useful solutions that endure and serve others, start out as abstract ideas.

You are the strongest link in the chain.

Your Gold strength for creating stability through solid dedication is motivated through your Green need to retain, advance, and use knowledge and information correctly, for the benefit of everyone. You organize, categorize, correct, maintain and utilize appropriate information (and practices) to create the stability and durability that people and organizations require, in order to be successful. You have a strong ethical nature that ensures that you use information that is true and applicable. Your dedication to others ensures that no one will have to wait, for your clear input or proper direction. Whether

The Color Guide to Life
© Erica W. Lowry & Don Lowry, 2014. www.donlowry.com

your knowledge is stored in your mind, in your files, on your hard drive, in the cloud, or on your bookshelves—others can count on you to find answers, expeditiously.

Your mind is more capable than any machine, at locating, organizing, and providing necessary, correct information and direction. You prioritize your thoughts and knowledge expertly, and you deliver individualized, detailed information and plans. You yourself lead a life that is strictly guided by the high ethical and moral standards that you set for yourself. If you ever have an occasional inner-conflict (which is rare), it's due to your need to adhere to traditional, trustworthy information and practices, and your need to create better, new information and more efficient practices.

As a Gold/Green/Orange/Blue, you use your work ethic and your store of knowledge to take concrete action, to get concrete results. If you're not the one taking action, you support those that do, by providing what they need. Your Orange enhances your Gold by making you a hands-on participant, and your Orange enhances your Green by making you more open to changes of plan. Your need to do things by the book is enhanced by a need to do it now. Your pale Blue signifies that you could possibly be more patient with others—and you'd do well to acknowledge others, for their contribution.

Preventing and Resolving Conflict

Conflict is caused when one's needs are not being met, and/or when it feels that one's values are being dishonored. Since True Colors so clearly describes our different needs and values, it makes understanding conflict much easier.

Every conflict has its very specific circumstances, but most everyday conflicts boil down to some version of the natural conflicts between the Colors.

You may also find that your Second Color is in conflict with someone else's Primary Color, because that set of values is also very important to you, as Second Color values are to everyone.

On the following pages, you'll see what needs and values of yours, directly conflict with the needs and values of each of the other Colors. When you and others can see that the central reason for your conflict is attributable to your True Colors—your natural differences—tempers usually calm down, because a way forward is apparent, in the clarity of understanding your natural differences.

It also bears repeating, that you have certain central characteristics in common, with each of the other Colors. Awareness of these commonalities can serve to point you in the right direction, toward a place of common ground.

To resolve a conflict, try to:

1. Calmly identify the basic needs not being met, and/or the basic values that feel dishonored.

2. Then, while you keep in mind your shared set of values,

3. Identify a relevant common goal (keep it as simple as you can).

4. Use the communication strategies suggested for each Color, to reach a compromise where each person gets at least some needs met, and some values honored.

Common Conflicts

GREENS	GOLDS
⇨ Like ingenuity and change	⇨ Prefer stability and traditional practices
⇨ Like to be independent	⇨ Like to follow the rules and cooperate with others
⇨ Like to see the "big picture"	⇨ Like to focus on the details, step-by-step
⇨ Value abstract ideas	⇨ Value practical ideas

Both Highly Value

⇨ An attention to important details

⇨ Privacy and hard work

⇨ Study and research

⇨ Keeping control of things

⇨ A determination to "get things right"

© Erica W. Lowry & Don Lowry, 2014. www.donlowry.com

Common Conflicts

BLUES	GREENS
⇨ Enjoy nurturing and supporting others	⇨ Like to remain independent
⇨ Rely on their strong intuition	⇨ Rely on logic and their intellect
⇨ Value togetherness and affection	⇨ Value time alone and restraint
⇨ Need communication and openness	⇨ Need privacy, and time to think

 # Both Highly Value

⇨ Abstract ideas

⇨ Idealism—new ideas for a brighter future

⇨ Intuition, and its application to life situations

⇨ Each of us making original, unique contributions

⇨ A tendency toward curiosity about the nature of human beings, resulting in many shared interests, such as psychology, philosophy, history, drama, art, anthropology —any subject area that offers a deeper understanding of human nature

© Erica W. Lowry & Don Lowry, 2014. www.donlowry.com

Common Conflicts

ORANGES	GOLDS
⇨ Like to bend the rules	⇨ Prefer to follow them
⇨ Like to be spontaneous	⇨ Like to be reliable, prefer consistency
⇨ Value risk-taking	⇨ Value the reduction of risk
⇨ Enjoy getting lots of attention	⇨ Prefer modesty

 # Both Highly Value

⇨ Very clear rules that make sense
⇨ Concrete action that has a real result that everyone understands
⇨ An admiration for things that have a wide, traditional appeal, that everyone understands
⇨ Being useful to one's family, organization, and community
⇨ A clear understanding of good versus evil

Common Conflicts

GREENS	ORANGES
⇨ Prefer privacy	⇨ Like to be center-stage
⇨ Like to think things through before taking action	⇨ Like to "do it now", love to take risks, and to make a "big impact"
⇨ Need to be competent, and to be regarded as such	⇨ Love a crowd to experiment with, and make changes on the fly
⇨ Tend to think in abstract terms	⇨ like things to be very concrete

 # Both Highly Value

⇨ Variety
⇨ Independence and Freedom
⇨ Creativity & Inventiveness
⇨ Flexibility
⇨ Changes to status quo when needed

© Erica W. Lowry & Don Lowry, 2014. www.donlowry.com

Common Conflicts

BLUES	GOLDS
➪ Value imagination and intuition	➪ Value practical, step-by-step guidelines
➪ Like to have the communication lines always open	➪ Prefer to communicate when necessary
➪ Tend to forgive a little rule-bending	➪ See rule-bending as rule-breaking
➪ Value lots of affection, any time, anywhere	➪ Reserve affection for appropriate moments
➪ Love to nurture all that is unique and original	➪ Like to maintain all that is stable and traditional

 # Both Highly Value

➪ Service to Others
➪ Cooperation
➪ Caring for family & community
➪ Honesty & sincerity
➪ Politeness

© Erica W. Lowry & Don Lowry, 2014. www.donlowry.com

Common Conflicts

ORANGES	BLUES
⇨ Often think teasing is affectionate	⇨ See teasing as cruel
⇨ Take risks, and like to "shake things up" once in a while	⇨ Never want to risk hurting anyone in any way
⇨ Bend the rules, which sometimes results in bending the truth	⇨ Forgiveness of bent rules is OK; but bending or lack of truth is not OK
⇨ Take immediate physical action to solve problems	⇨ Apply compassion and imagination to solve problems
⇨ Often think conflict is healthy	⇨ Think conflict is the greatest stressor there is

Both Highly Value

⇨ Creativity

⇨ Enthusiasm

⇨ Generosity

⇨ Everyone making a unique contribution

⇨ Optimism

© Erica W. Lowry & Don Lowry, 2014. www.donlowry.com

The Real, True, Secret Story Of the Origin of "Temperament" and "True Colors"

In 2009, Don suggested I write a new piece outlining the history of Temperament and True Colors. I thought to myself, *this subject has been fully explored since the 1980s—what more is there to say?* But by 2009, we had new research tools that we didn't have in previous decades, so I thought I'd see what a new, in-depth online look into Temperament would reveal. Lo and behold, some amazing new discoveries came my way—from the very origins of Temperament, to its ancient use in Athenian Comedy, to some jaw-dropping news about William Shakespeare, on stage playing one of the Temperaments—and finally, to new questions about the very existence of Temperament in a human being, from Carl G. Jung. Jung was the originator, of modern Type and Temperament Theory, and his insights on his posthumously published, best-selling "Red Book" (W.W. Norton, 2009) offer new, beguiling ideas about the origins of "personality."

The story of Temperament and True Colors is a fascinating one, beginning with the long oral history of storytelling—of Gods and Goddesses, in Ancient Greece.

It Wasn't Necessarily Who You Thought

The origin of classifying individuals according to four personality types is nearly as ancient as Western civilization, and it did not necessarily begin with Hippocrates, as is commonly believed. The notion of personality differences as something quantifiable (rather than purely ineffable or merely inherited, a result of the personalities of one's ancestors), began with the pre-Socratic philosopher **Empedocles (490 B.C.— 430 B.C.).** He was a citizen of Agrigentum, a Greek colony in Sicily. He proposed the still well-known theory that the world and its contents (including us human beings) were comprised of the four elements, **Earth, Air, Fire, and Water**. In his epic poem, "On Nature," he stated that these elements were

© Erica W. Lowry & Don Lowry, 2014. www.donlowry.com

ruled by the gods **Persephone, Zeus, Hades, and Hera** — whose personalities happened to be an ideal representation of the characteristics of those four elements, respectively—which align with the later understanding of four "Temperaments." [1]

Those four gods and their very distinct personalities didn't come out of thin air, naturally—they were fictional characters that were based upon very real, natural human personality traits, representing a long oral tradition that inspired the first known work of Western literature, "The Iliad," by **Homer (approx. 850 B.C.[2]).**

One must consider that the oral history of the gods and goddesses, and the written work of Homer, influenced ancient Greek society, mores, and philosophy (including the philosophies of Empedocles and Hippocrates) the way that storytelling and "the media" influences us, today. Empedocles' new theory set the stage for a culture that believed that the nature of one's individual being, i.e. why we are the way we are, was something attributable to qualities that were *quantifiable*, defined by only four elements, with only four possible influences—in this case, gods and goddesses. Empedocles wrote, "Those in whom the elements are mingled in equal or almost equal proportions . . . are the most intelligent and have the most exact perceptions."

This theory of the four natural elements comprising all that is became a standard dogma for the next two thousand years.

---

1 Zeus, the "god of gods", the visionary who lived on Mount Olympus and impassively ruled every corner of the planet, would have been "Air", which would be "Green", in True Colors language, or "NT" in Myers-Briggs Type Indicator language; his wife Hera, by all accounts an emotional person, very sentimental and merciful (yet wrathful, when betrayed), would have represented "Water", which would be represented by "Blue", or "NF", in the Myers-Briggs Type Indicator's understanding; Persephone, who traveled back and forth between the underworld and the natural world in order to preserve balance and her own loyalties, would be "Earth", which would be represented by "Gold", or "SJ", in MBTI language; and Hades, her husband - the overseer of the underworld, would have been "Fire", which would be represented within True Colors' metaphor, as the color "Orange", or "SP", in the language of Myers-Briggs Type Indicator.

2   Scholars do not all agree on the date of Homer's existence. Some place him a century earlier, some a century later.

According to **Aristotle (384 B.C—322 B.C)**, Empedocles died at the age of 60, as "The father of Rhetoric." (Empedocles was the last Greek philosopher to record his theories, in verse. Back then, "rhetoric" meant the art of writing and speaking eloquently, not the art of avoiding the truth, which is what it often means today!) Interestingly, Empedocles also theorized that all human knowledge is explained by the principle that the elements in things outside of us are perceived and understood by the corresponding elements within ourselves— as in, "perception is reality." (Or to look at it another way, "like attracts like.")

The concepts of Empedocles, due to his fame in Western Europe, were well known by **Hippocrates (470 B.C—370 B.C.)**, the pre-eminent Greek philosopher and physician, who is known as "The Father of Medicine." Hippocrates originated medicine as a profession, and is known not only for "The Hippocratic Oath" but also for his many methods of prognosis, some of which are still in use today, in pulmonary medicine. Hippocrates described what he observed and theorized as four distinct types of human Temperaments (or "humours," or personalities), caused by what he believed were the effects on an individual caused by the levels of four different bodily fluids: black bile, yellow bile, phlegm, and blood. During his lifetime in Greece, human dissection was considered to be a sacrilege, so Hippocrates didn't have direct access to the internal mechanisms of the human body. However, it was Hippocrates who rejected the standard notion (theorized by Empedocles and others) that disease was a punishment by the gods—he theorized that disease was rather due to an internal imbalance in these four fluids, which was evident through a person's "Temperament." He called these four Temperaments Choleric (emotional and sensitive), Phlegmatic (impassive and judgmental), Melancholic (someone who's a natural worrier and protector), and Sanguine (fiery and spirited).

The individual's personality indicated what sort of fluid-imbalance, and therefore illness, he or she might have.

Hippocrates summed up his theory well when he said, *"It's more important to understand what sort of person has a disease, than what sort of disease a person has."*—In other words, Hippocrates considered an individual's personality to be an inherent indicator, of what might be causing his or her illness.

Of course, at the time "personality" was not understood as an aspect of "psychology," a science unto itself, separate from biology. "Psychology" wouldn't exist for another 2000 years. Hippocrates (and Empedocles) were concerned with physical illness; mental illness was considered a manifestation of physical illness.

Hippocrates' assignment of four "Temperaments" to describe our "ill" personality tendencies found their way to a megaphone—Athenian Comedy, which demonstrated our different personalities, when we behave in all the misbegotten ways that humans do.

Temperament Makes Comedy Funnier, Forever

Aristotle (384 - 322 B.C) was familiar with the advances made by Hippocrates, as were all notable philosophers at the time, in Greece. The successor to Aristotle's position at his Lyceum in Athens was his immensely prolific student, **Theophrastus (371 B.C.—287 B.C.).** Theophrastus' philosophical and scientific interests and published works were wide-ranging, including works in biology and physics, however one of his most important works was his booklet, "The Characters," which was based on Hippocrates' work in Temperament. This booklet, describing 30 characters, was the first recorded attempt at a systematic, detailed description of different, distinct Temperaments, which has resulted in the term, "the character sketch." Luckily, we still have it, and it's available to everyone for free. Indeed, Theophrastus' detailed descriptions of the wide variety of personalities within the combinations of Temperament are hilarious, farcical ren-

© Erica W. Lowry & Don Lowry, 2014. www.donlowry.com

ditions that are starkly recognizable as the worst possible expression of our faults in everyday life. (To download Theophrastus' book for free, go to Archive.org and search for "Characters of Theophrastus." I highly recommend it.)

If you're familiar with True Colors, you can try to guess the distinct True Colors Spectrum, of each of Theophrastus' Characters. Of all the 24 possible varieties of Spectrum, not one is missing—however quite unlike True Colors, Theophrastus positively thrashes every human foible, in the name of farce.

One of Theophrastus' friends was a gifted comedic playwright, named **Menander (341 B.C.—290 B.C.)**, who was the author of more than a hundred Athenian Comedies. He took the prize at the Lenaia festival in Greece eight times (that's sort of like getting eight Tony Awards). He was one of the most popular playwrights of antiquity; he utilized Theophrastus' concept of "Character," to revolutionize the ways that Athenian Comedy was written and performed.

Previously, Greek Comedy had relied on a form of entertainment that lampooned local officials, satirized local and political scandals, and utilized song and verse to get story across to audiences. Instead, Menander utilized the "Characters" derived from his friend Theophrastus' "The Characters", to create spoken comedy that was more universal, and less local. His plays reached a much broader audience, because the Temperaments he brought to life were familiar to everyone in every audience. He used personal love stories for some of his plots, which was a new story-mine for Athenian theater. His work formed the foundation of Athenian "New Comedy," which exaggerated the characters' Temperaments to create hilarious stories about everyday lives. Though nearly all of Menander's plays have been lost, his use of "the character sketch" based on Temperament was copied by other playwrights. This signified the height of Athenian theater, which has influenced much of Western European literature and theater.

This brilliant use of the understanding of Temperament to create stories that everyone in an audience can relate to might have been lost, if **George Chapman (1559-1634)**, had not unearthed this method, and used it again England, on the popular stage. The first Elizabethan playwright to experiment with the "Characters" of Theophrastus and Menander, George Chapman was a classical Greek scholar, playwright, and translator most noted for the first English translations of Homer's "Iliad" and "Oddyssey" (a tremendous feat, bringing the earliest literature to the known world). In 1597 Chapman wrote the play, "An Humorous Days' Mirth," which created the vogue for what's now known as "A Comedy of Humours." These "Humours," were Hippocrates four "Temperaments."

In fact the word "humour," to mean "personality," or "character," was derived from Hippocrates' referral to "fluids," in his theory regarding the body's fluids as influencing our Temperament: The word "liquid," in the Latin which Hippocrates spoke, is pronounced "humour."

But it was the playwright **Ben Jonson (June 11, 1572-August 6, 1637)** who became the champion of this form of theater, utilizing Hippocrates' four Temperaments. Jonson's most famous play in this genre is "Every Man in His Humour," produced in 1598. Indeed Ben Jonson, in his day, was more popular than William Shakespeare, who's since far, far eclipsed him. Jonson and Shakespeare both worked within the same small theatrical sphere, in England, at the same time. Actors and playwrights often assisted one another during this period, as they very often still do, since theatre is a rarefied, underpaid field.

And so it was none other than **William Shakespeare, (baptized April 26, 1564—April 23, 1616)**, who played the part of "Kno'well," in the earliest productions of "Every Man in His Humour." If you happen to read the play, you'd discover that Kno'well's character is *Gold* (rather than Green, as his name might suggest). His name refers to the character's

© Erica W. Lowry & Don Lowry, 2014. www.donlowry.com

unbending, "know-it-all" stance on morality, social propriety, and familial and financial responsibilities. It's comedy, of course, so Kno'well's characteristics are not only exaggerated, they inevitably subvert his own purposes.

Ben Jonson succinctly summarized the theory of human Temperament, as it is played out in life and in theater:

"Some one peculiar quality
Doth so possess a man, that it doth draw
All his affects, his spirits, and his powers—

In their confluctions, all to run one way."

In Europe and America, this form of comedy—of using the "character sketch," that is, a formula for basic, universal characters—is evident in several of the most popular modern and contemporary situation comedies: I Love Lucy, All in the Family, M.A.S.H., Fawlty Towers, Seinfeld, Friends, and Sex in the City are some examples of the characterization of the four Temperaments in 20th century television. The writers for these shows (knowingly or not) put their finger on a universal pulse; they included characters that spoke to every possible viewer. It's a formula that will likely always be around, whether or not writers are familiar with Temperament, because it's representative of the different ways that people really are— even in an exaggerated, farcical form. (We've all met a Lucy, or a Kramer, or both!)

In Medicine, Temperament Becomes Doctrine —Then Heresy—Then Quackery

During the pre-Christian years, and into the **Middle Ages (which lasted between the 5th and 15th centuries throughout Europe)**, and well into the **Rennaisance (late 15th century Italy, through 18th century Europe)** the use of Hippocrates' medical diagnosis of the four Temperaments for the purposes of assessing illness was the traditional practice throughout Europe. The practice had also expanded into Egypt and Mesopotamia (what is now Iraq).

During the Pre-Christian era, Hippocrates' medical infamy had been further established by **Galen (129-200 C.E)**, who was also a philosopher and physician, and who was the personal physician to **Marcus Aurelius (April 26, 121 C.E.—March 26, 180 C.E.)**, the Emperor, residing in Rome. Galen was the most prolific author in Western Europe, during his lifetime (producing over 600 volumes). Galen saw Hippocrates as nearly "divine," and Galen used not just Hippocrates' theories of Temperament in his prognosis and treatment of patients, but used all of Hippocrates' other practices, as well.

Galen was so well-known, that his legacy created what must have seemed at the time a permanent tradition among physicians, who institutionalized many of Hippocrates' and Galens' views throughout Western Europe, lasting for over a millenia.

However in the early 1500s (as the Middle Ages were just beginning to wane, finally giving way to The Rennaisance), a Swiss physician, also a philosopher and alchemist, by the name of **Philippus Paracelsus (1493-1541)** utilized both Hyppocrates' and Galens' doctrines, while at the same time burning their books, to signify his own independence.

Paracelsus pioneered the use of chemicals and metals in the practice of medicine, and was the first to discuss the existence of "the unconscious," in his writings. During the strict enforcement of Christianity during the Middle Ages, when the religious beliefs of Hippocrates and Galen were condemned, Paracelsus was an influential genius—who was able to create social change by utilizing the ideas of Hippocrates and Galen, while still adhering to the mores of his time. He used his own language for Hippocrates' Temperaments, saying that the four natures observed by Hippocrates were influenced by four kinds of "spirits," which were Nymphs, Sylphs, Gnomes, and Salamanders, each of which denoted a distinctly different set of behaviors in human beings. The concept of using spirit-names was born of Paracelsus' worldview, common in Western Europe, which incorporated some pagan beliefs, even during the Middle Ages. (This use of "spirits" to denote Temperament reminds one of Empedocles' nomination of two "gods" and two "goddesses," to represent the character of each of the four elements that he believed comprised our being.) Paracelcus' "spirits," representing human personalities, presented a "pagan" alternative to the then-punitive doctrine of the Christian Church, which didn't give "personality" an inch

© Erica W. Lowry & Don Lowry, 2014. www.donlowry.com

of legitimacy.   And so while "psychology" would not exist for another four centuries, in his writings on the "unconscious" Paracelsus was the first to make strides toward understanding human nature from a more psychological perspective.

During the Renaissance, the Hippocratic notion of Temperament became unpopular, due to dramatic advances in science, including anatomy, astronomy, and geography—not to mention all of the advances that were made in the arts. **Leonardo da Vinci (April 15, 1453—May 2, 1519)** drew detailed sketches of human internal organs, which showed beyond the shadow of a doubt that disease was not caused by an imbalance in bodily fluids. Most ancient medical philosophies were, for the time being, ignored due their discredit in the findings of human biology.

A New Branch of Medicine—And A Posthumous Revelation, from Dr. Carl G. Jung

It wasn't until 1921, when the Swiss phycologist **Dr. Carl Gustav Jung (July 26, 1875—June 6, 1961)** published his book, "Psychological Types," that Temperament Theory entered the new realm, of scientific psychological theory. His book reaffirmed the ancient understanding of four fixed patterns of behavior (which to this day are ascribed to Hippocrates, rather than Empedocles), which could be used to better understand human beings. Jung proposed that each of us is born with a particular disposition, and that each one of us strives to express our "truest self" as either a *Thinker,* a *Feeler*, a *Sensor*, or an *Intuitor*. Jung was a colleague of **Dr. Sigmund Freud (May 6, 1856—September 23, 1939)** however Dr. Freud and Dr. Jung parted ways on such matters as Jung's concept of the "Collective Unconscious," which is now recognized as a worthy theory among metaphysicians, many psychologists, and some physicists. Jung spent his lifetime theorizing and practicing many new concepts that are today still used in psychoanalysis, art, and literature: the concepts of

© Erica W. Lowry & Don Lowry, 2014. www.donlowry.com

Anima and Animus (which symbolize the archetypal man in the mind of a woman, and the archetypal woman in the mind of a man), Synchronicity (unusual coincidence occurring at signal moments), and the concept of introversion and extraversion (Jung's definition varies in some important ways from the current, popular notion[3]). Jung's theory of Temperament is also correlated to his in-depth study of "Archetype," which he said were permanent, stable symbols of different types and stages of basic human nature, that exist in the substratum of every human mind, or the Collective Unconscious.

In discussing his posthumously-published "The Red Book," (W.W. Norton, pub. October 2009) Jung made clear that all of his philosophies in the field of psychology were born of personal experiences that he had had during a sixteen-year period of deep inner wandering into the farthest realms of his own subconscious, wherein he experienced difficult confrontations with images and personalities within his own psyche. These sixteen years of experiences are all recorded in words and masterful artwork, in "The Red Book," which he exempted from being published during his lifetime, because he was concerned that it would undermine all of his work among professional colleagues. (The Jung family would not allow the book to be published, until 2009.)

Jung was convinced that aspects of mind arising from a person's subconscious affecting one's behavior (i.e., universal Archetypes, and one's own Temperament) were aspects that originated and arose from the Collective Unconscious, rather than merely inherited from parents (and thereafter developed

---

3 Jung was very apprehensive about the simplification of the terms "introvert" and extravert" as used by Type practitioners and others, as their use reduced (and popularized) the terminology into the categorization of people into two categories, which he felt was incorrect. He described introversion and extraversion as dynamic tendencies that were complex, which took into consideration not only the inherent personality, but the personality at different stages, and in different social contexts which affected the expressed personality as one with more or less "introverted" or "extraverted" behaviors. In True Colors' language, for instance, a "Green" person may be "introverted" at a party, but "extraverted" in a classroom setting. According to Don Lowry, our "values in context" are a primary driver for whether or not we feel comfortable fully expressing our natural strengths and motivations.

© Erica W. Lowry & Don Lowry, 2014. www.donlowry.com

during a person's lifetime).

That idea—the idea that one's character or Temperament is something born of the Collective Unconscious, that is, *everyone's* unconscious, is quite extraordinary to think of.

It harkens back, again, to the notion that "gods and goddesses" dictate our character, although in this case, the "gods and goddesses". . . are us, or at least the part of us that we know the least about. It makes sense, if you consider how the sets of characteristics within the Temperaments are always within alignment in an individual, and almost always predictive of behavior.

What can manifest any kind of universal, near-perfect alignment in human nature, but something that human beings do not control or understand?

About the importance of his "Red Book," Jung stated, "The years... when I pursued the inner images, were the most important time of my life. Everything else is to be derived from this. It began at that time, and the later details hardly matter anymore. My entire life consisted in elaborating what had burst forth from the unconscious and flooded me like an enigmatic stream and threatened to break me. That was the stuff and material for more than only one life. Everything later was merely the outer classification, scientific elaboration, and the integration into life. But the numinous beginning, which contained everything, was then."

Into the Mainstream . . . and Back Into the Footlights, After 380 Years

Jung's Temperament Theory was not adaptable for everyday use until the relatively recent development of the Myers-Briggs Type Indicator, which was created in 1956 by **Katherine Briggs (1875-1968)** and her daughter, **Isabel Briggs-Myers (October 18, 1897—May 5,**

1980). Their work sparked a renewed interest in the field of personality theory. Myers and Briggs expanded Jung's theory to encompass sixteen "Type-indicators," which identified dominant "Type" behaviors in order, and incorporated either "introversion" or "extraversion." (In fact, Jung was wary of such simplification, of "introversion" and "extraversion.") What started out as a parlor game that Katherine Briggs and Isabel Briggs-Myers introduced to their friends, became a very popular tool for the use of psychologists with their patients, and for human resource departments seeking to better understand employees. (And although in all likelihood she probably didn't know about Theophrastus' "Characters," since it has never been discussed in Psychology, Isabel Briggs-Myers used the psychological types to form the characters in her novels, "Murder Yet to Come" and "Give Me Death.")

Late 20th-century psychologist **Dr. David Keirsey (August 31, 1921—July 30, 2013)**, in his best-selling book of 1978, "Please Understand Me," explains the correlation between Jung's four Temperaments and the sixteen Myers/Briggs Type Indicators. Keirsey labels the four Temperaments Apollonian, Promethean, Epimethean, and Dionysian (harkening back to Hippocrates' Greece). In Dr. Keirsey's book, there is a detailed questionnaire that readers take, to discover one's "Temperament," so that with the results, one could understand one's self to a higher degree. This, in turn, helps to improve one's self-esteem. (Dr. Keirsey's book, "Please Understand Me II," published in 1998, is viewed as a classic in the genre of "self-help.")

In 1978, **Don Lowry (born May 18, 1936)** was a successful businessman in education, with a background in teaching biology and athletic coaching. When Lowry read Dr. Kiersey's first book, it happened that Lowry's youngest brother Bill, who had been in Lowry's care, had just committed suicide. This very tragic event caused Lowry to decide to give up what he had been doing as a businessman, and instead find a way to make the information in Temperament Theory much more

© Erica W. Lowry & Don Lowry, 2014. www.donlowry.com

accessible to people, especially young people. Lowry by then had had his first child, Donnell, and he wanted to find a way to create a more peaceful, cooperative world for his daughter, at a time when there was so much civil violence and unrest in America. Dr. Kiersey's home was quite close to where Lowry lived, and Lowry decided to visit Dr. Kiersey, to see what he could learn. With a shared, intense passion for improving the lives of people, Dr. Kiersey became Lowry's mentor, and Lowry his protégé. Lowry was convinced that all people, regardless of age, culture, or background, could benefit from knowing about the fundamental principles of personality—they could learn to understand themselves better, and also learn to appreciate and support individual differences. He felt that even children and teenagers could benefit greatly, from this deeper self-understanding.

Lowry further simplified the language used to discuss personality, to replace the rather complicated (and sometimes difficult to remember, in the case of the MBTI) labels with a simple, modern metaphor: colors. Blue, Green, Gold, and Orange would be used to describe the four Temperaments. He chose the colors very carefully, after studying the associations of each color within various cultures and shared experiences:

- Green represents the natural life of earth—plants, signifying growth, complexity, and expansion;

- Blue represents the oceans and the sky, signifying depth, flowing movement, and association with "the heavens" (spirituality);

- Orange represents fire, signifying excitement, action, and spontaneity;

- Gold represents the earth's vital resources, signifying solidity, value, and protection.

He chose to call his system "True Colors," after the popular euphemism "showing one's true colors"—an apt metaphor for "showing one's true self," which is what understanding and appreciating our own personality helps us to do.

Here's a secret, shared by Don. It's a little-known fact that for a little more than a year, "Gold" was originally called "Brown," the color of earth, signifying permanence and sustainability. But after these types of people told Lowry that they very much disliked this color metaphor for themselves, Lowry chose "Gold"—as in "Good as Gold," and "Solid Gold," which Gold folks liked very much.

Lowry knew that he could not do what he wanted to do, as quickly as he wanted to do it, through a long, written self-assessment. He realized that high-"Orange" Types would resist this type of written "test," which would skew his data for whole populations. He also knew that many young children would not sit through a long questionnaire. (And by the way, he also knew that many "Green" folks would bridle at participating in an event called a "workshop," where they would have to share their own personal experiences with a group of people. This type of person is very private.) Don wanted to reach everybody, of every Color—adults and children alike.

It occurred to him to use comedy entertainment, where he would use characters to demonstrate the four types; and he would use farce, a genre of satirical comedy, to further highlight the differences between the four Types—the four Colors.

With no background in philosophy, literature, or the history of theater, Lowry had of course never heard of Menander, much less Theophrastus, much less Ben Johnson's "Comedy of Humours." This theatrical branch of Temperament had never been discussed in psychological literature, because psychology is viewed strictly as a branch of medicine. Nor had Dr. Keirsey heard of Theophrastus' having assigned Temperaments to dramatic "characters," or Menander's use of those characters in Athenian New Comedy, to create the foundation for one of the basic formulas for Western theater.

The Color Guide to Life
© Erica W. Lowry & Don Lowry, 2014. www.donlowry.com

In fact, Dr. Keirsey doubted that Lowry could accomplish such a thing as create theater based upon Temperament; but Lowry felt instinctively that this was the best way to bring the healing concepts of Temperament to all. Little did Lowry know, that using these universal concepts in theatrical farce, would be such a resounding success.

In fact, it was a risk. Don had no professional supporters—and so he wrote, produced, and performed the show by himself, playing all four parts—without knowing what the outcome would be, for audiences.

To further assist audiences in recognizing the "Colors" within themselves, Lowry created a playbill containing four "Character Cards," depicting characteristics of the four Colors. So that audience members could understand the cards very quickly and in a playful manner (as there is very limited time, between the moment when an audience is seated, and when the curtain rises), Lowry used vivid pictures on one side, showing symbols and mimes to depict aspects of the four personality types, and he used highly condensed verbiage on the other side of the cards, to quickly describe the types.

The use of four colors served as an easy "language" for audiences to immediately begin describing and talking about one's "True Colors," one's "true self"—and the advent of the use of pictures (not just words) made the Temperaments very quick and easy and to understand. The use of cards, which reminds people of a game, made self-understanding interactive and fun. Lowry's playbill instructed audiences to sort the cards from "Most Like Me" to "Least Like Me," with the understanding that we each have all four Colors within us. Then, audience members were to watch the show, to see which character was most like themselves. (Of course, they recognized on stage everyone else they knew, as well.)

This was the first time that people of all ages had easy access to the complex theories of Temperament, and it was the first time that people could accurately decide upon their own Temperament themselves, without being "told" by an expert. With True Colors, Lowry put self-understanding squarely into the hands of the individual.

By 1980, Lowry had developed "The Game of Games," an entertaining play that was performed by four actors. Audience members could not only "watch themselves" onstage, acting out various comedic life-scenarios, the audience could interact with each of the four characters, to further enhance and enjoy their newfound self-understanding.

His shows were an enormous success. Therapists sent patients to see the show, so that they could clarify their self-view and their relationships. Teachers could recognize students, and vice-versa; parents could recognize their children, and vice-versa. Every audience member could watch, and laugh about—and forgive—their many differences. In 1984, Dr. Keirsey sent Lowry a congratulatory letter, admitting that he didn't think that it could be done.

From the office of David Keirsey, Ph.D.

Professor Emeritus
California State University
Fullerton, CA 92634

Dear Don,

I must congratulate you on your success in producing a topical stage play that does not do injustice to a most complex and therefore difficult topic. You may recall that when you first essayed to put the temperaments on stage I evinced some skepticism and cautioned you to avoid mere cartoons of the temperament types. I believed at the time cartoons of the types would be misleading and that the consequence would be that the theory of temperaments would be subjected to ridicule. You persisted. I stand corrected.

The Color Guide to Life
© Erica W. Lowry & Don Lowry, 2014. www.donlowry.com

It was your choice of humor as the vehicle for the caricatures that saved the day, indeed, made the day. The play is fun. People can identify with the characters. They can see themselves on stage and they can laugh at themselves and consequently cease to take themselves so seriously. Of course a few skits cannot possibly inform the viewer on the depth and complexity of temperament theory. But informing cannot have been the intent of the play. Its function rather is to intrigue the viewer with two ideas: that people are fundamentally different and that these differences are good. It may well be that many, given this witty introduction to the study of human differences, will take up the study.

I not only congratulate you, but I thank you for your achievement in advancing the public's awareness of the theory of temperaments and the National Association for Psychological Type.

Sincerely,

David W. Keirsey
10/7/84

Lowry's next foray was an ABC pilot, "What Are Your True Colors?" But his greatest success was in live theater, due to the interactive nature of the plays.

Lowry understood that the generic use of "color" as a language gave people a shared fluency, across cultures and languages, to discuss and apply a general "Temperament" of any human ideology, event, or societal system, as it reflected the values of those responsible for an ideology, an event, or a system. Understanding True Colors enables us to recognize a "Gold school," an "Orange party," a "Blue restaurant," or a "Green idea." The use of color broadened the lens of Temperament, to apply to everything.

This method wasn't without its strong detractors in the

© Erica W. Lowry & Don Lowry, 2014. www.donlowry.com

Temperament community, who felt that lay-people were not capable of understanding such complex information, much less have the ability to decide for themselves their own Temperament. Lowry decided to go his own way, because he felt very strongly that if Temperament is a true theory, then everyone would be able to recognize their own Temperament. He felt that the "black boxes" (of scientific questionnaires, where one needs an expert to "interpret") weren't needed, for people to be able to recognize themselves. (In fact, the validity of True Colors' methodology bears out in scientific research.[4])

Lowry adapted the show for schools—he called the show "Discovering the Best in All of Us." Seeing the value of entertainment as a tool to educate, he created several simple, powerful, entertaining workshop processes[5] that enable participants to discover their greatest strengths, needs, values, joys, and stressors—and processes that enable participants to deeply appreciate one another and immediately apply what they've learned, within their personal lives, their communities, and their workplaces. These processes were expressed in his Facilitator's Guide "Stride With Pride," first published in 1980, and later copyrighted. Lowry began to certify professional trainers, to facilitate his workshops. His workbook that accompanies his workshop processes, "The Keys to Personal Success," has since sold over a million copies. His invention became much more than a personality assessment—it became a way to dramatically enhance lives and relationships.

Lowry brought True Colors to inner city schools, community centers, and public agencies, and he began to train educators in how to use this exciting new tool within their classrooms, with the new materials he'd authored for teachers, "The Keys to Successful Teaching," and "The Action and Communication Guide." (In these books, True Colors is used as an effective Learning Styles model.) He

---

4   "Reliability and Validity of True Colors," by Judith A. Wichard, Ph.D., June 2006.
5   "The Discovery Process," "The Brightening Process," "The Ideal Process," "The Blending Process," "The 'Commercial' Process," and other processes.

created systemic programs for schools and organizations, which involve all participants in learning and applying the benefits of self- and mutual understanding and appreciation. In his first school-wide program (in 1989-1999), 350 schools in Tennessee participated, wherein everyone understood and used True Colors in every context—all staff, students, teachers, parents, and the community participated. The use of True Colors Shows was key to the program's success, in bringing all participants together in a common understanding. Don enlisted students to write comedy scripts based on True Colors, which were performed by students for the community. These inspired students brought the whole community onto its feet, not just to cheer for the students, but for their own newfound understanding of one another. True Colors shows offer an uncanny revelation that people use every day, for the rest of their lives.

It should be noted, that until this writing (November 2009), the history of the use of Temperament in theater, dating back to the "New Comedy" of ancient Athens, has never been touched upon in any comprehensive history of Psychological Temperament, because in modern times, the primary focus of the study of Temperament (until the advent of True Colors) had been strictly psychological. True Colors is the only Temperament model that embodies both the psychological and the theatrical, and is based firmly in the theatrical.

True Colors programs have been adapted by both Don Lowry and several authors of True Colors products, for extensive use in Health and Wellness[6], Teaching and Learning, Leadership, Conflict Prevention and Resolution, Sales, Teambuilding, Diversity, Career Development, Family Relationships, Love Relationships, Criminal Justice, and

---

6 "In 2015, the American Psychological Association's Center for Organizational Excellence chose a True Colors-based program, "Color Me Healthy" for a national award given to organizations for excellence in improving employee health and well-being, while enhancing organizational performance and productivity. "Color Me Healthy" was created by True Colors Certified Facilitator Kim Kent, for the company, "Team Horner."

© Erica W. Lowry & Don Lowry, 2014. www.donlowry.com

Coaching. It is currently used in diverse settings in nearly every walk of life—from executive boardrooms to kindergarten classrooms, with a wide range of client groups that include many Fortune 100 and 500 companies and government agencies; it is used by therapists and professional coaches worldwide, and hundreds of schools and universities in various countries. True Colors is translated into thirteen languages.

Don Lowry, the Creator and Founder of True Colors®, True Colors Entertainment, and the True Colors Workshop Processes, resides in Laguna Niguel, California, with his wife Erica. He is Green/Orange/Blue/Gold.

About the Author

Erica WalkingStick Lowry lives with her husband Don Lowry in Laguna Niguel, California. She has authored a wide array of True Colors books, scripts, games, systemic programs and courses in Education and Emotional Wellness for all ages, including an in-depth application of True Colors in love relationships, "True LoveStyles." She expanded the four Types in True Colors, to provide a detailed understanding of all 24 possible True Colors Spectrums, in "TrueColors 24." This model is employed in her program for assisting Health Coaches and Executive Coaches to work with individuals, "Coaching Colors." She has written a book for leaders and educators, "Six Levels of Distress in Four Colors: Causes, Symptoms, and Healing Strategies" which provides a specialized guide for dealing with stress, for each Color. She has a daughter, Sadie, who was co-author with her, of "The Colorbot Book for Boys and Girls," True Colors' application used with children ages 4-8. Erica is the author of "Flying Your True Colors for True Success," the foundational book for high school students. She is currently writing a book based upon her program for couples and singles, which will be entitled "The Color Guide to Love."

Contact Erica Lowry at Erica@donlowry.com

Contact Don Lowry at Don@donlowry.com

The Color Guide to Life
© Erica W. Lowry & Don Lowry, 2014. www.donlowry.com